PARIS around the CLOCK

© 1995 éditions Parigramme/CPL
59, rue Beaubourg, 75003 Paris

Jacques-Louis Delpal

Photographs by Jacques Lebar,
Martine Mouchy and Christian Sarramon

Translated from French by Nancy Bragard

Parigramme

Foreword

Paris day and night. On these one hundred square kilometers of high historic density, nearly two million two hundred thousand people (according to the last census) live in the heart of a gigantic and complex metropolis. The capital may lay still between the last and first metro, but only ever closes one eye. There are always men and women working in this city when other workers rest; there are always Parisians playing, reveling, laughing and clapping when the city quiets down, drowses and dreams.

Sometimes late, as if tired of counting time, the capital's clocks measure the daily routine at crossroads, on the pediments of monuments, of the City Hall and train stations. Noon to midnight, midnight to noon: the big pendulum of city life never stops. Every hour has its duties, its deadlines, its relaxation, its fun. There are twenty-four of them, not one more, but with as many nuances as there are quarter and half-hours.

Frédéric Chopin once said of the city that Montaigne proclaimed to dearly love, "Paris is whatever you want, right down to its spots and warts..." The bimillennial city, day after day, night after night, shuffles the thousands, the millions of lives with good cheer or rigor, captivating or holding captive, making even the fringe follow its urban rhythm, backwards if they choose. Between "good morning" and "good evening", between the first stirrings and the last yawns, Paris regulates its humdrum and whims by the clock. Schedules may suffer a setback here or there, depending on the job, the district, the mood...

This book portrays the many faces of Paris, at different angles, hour after hour. The day could be any day, at the end of spring or beginning of fall, under a slightly shifting sky. It's what you might call a promising day... that is, if you take the time to see what the weather's like, between suburban train station and office. This is Paris around the clock, sometimes to the tune of an accordion, other times to a work of contemporary music. The Paris in these pages is part routine and part festive, both hard working and vacationing. It speaks of the monotonous metro-job routine, but also of everyday's delightful, little pleasures, like an idle moment in a public garden. It depicts leisurely shopping among colorful stalls, as well as the rat race to catch a train; well-known restaurants along with casual pubs. It exalts the Pompidou Center, the exquisite Grand Louvre that France and her history gave to the capital. It recognizes the throngs of workers, like this enchanting artist of the night in her dressing room at the *Crazy Horse Saloon*.

The curtains rise. André Breton had set the alarm clock: "In the early morning hours, you must go up to the very top of the hill at Sacré-Cœur and watch the city slowly slip out of its gorgeous veils, before stretching its arms."

FIVE A.M.

Paris stirs... on the treshold between day and night

It's five o'clock, Paris awakens: to the French this is a familiar tune, hummed more often by the returning night-owl than by the early riser. The sun, rising on the left, has a long day ahead at this time of year before setting on the right. The Montmartre steps stand overlooking the sluggish city. It appears immense, blurred from this perspective, its early light still draped in shadows, not really belonging to humanity. And yet throngs of people are working, intent on their tasks, in twos, in threes. The bakers, the bartenders, those who open shop at dawn's first glow, have not yet turned out the neon lights of their late-night, early-morning job.

The day looks promising, but we'll get back to that. Now it's time to scurry about and finish the work started in pitch black, that of setting everything in place. An early-riser already at the bar counter orders a *café au lait*. Delivery trucks pass by. No traffic yet.

The Montmartre funicular dozes in its glass and metal berth, next to the cascade of steps and lawns, officially named Square Adolphe-Willette, in memory of the illustrator who grew up in the neighborhood. In a few hours, the panoramic trams, conceived by Roger Tallon who designed the famous TGV (bullet train), will swell with tourists. Below Sacré-Cœur, still a hesitant white, the zigzags of the rugged ascent quietly uncover a variety of roofs, domes and bell towers. A pink dust gently settles on the base of Montmartre, blurring the huge mass of the capital city and its awaiting districts. What a shame it's too early to get up; this is when Paris breathes, when its stones gently vibrate in the shadows for those rare souls who are up so early and who marvel at the ever-recurrent beginning. A heartless or tender city?

The day looks promising, but we'll get back to that. Dawn comes daily, yet it's always new. Already a honking car? Could be a flustered night-owl with his upside-down schedule, sounding off at the delivery trucks.

FIVE THIRTY A.M.

MORNING METRO BLUES...

The agent has just opened the sliding metal gates; no odors yet. There are always crowds of people at the terminuses, probably more at Saint-Denis-Basilique or Porte d'Orléans than at Porte Dauphine. Most of them are on their way to work, some are returning home. Lots of tennis shoes, few Vuitton bags. Five thirty on the dot: at the end of every line, a train shakes into motion. The regulars don't know how lucky they are: those who take the first metro never have the frustrated impression that later users have of just missing the previous one.

Drivers of line number eight need a full hour to travel from Créteil (suburb) to Balard (almost a suburb) or vice-versa. The line exaggerates the waving course of the Seine: a curve ascending up to République and Opéra, tumbling down the left bank through the Invalides and La Motte-Piquet-Grenelle where three lines, including the aerial one, come together, crossing over one another. The drivers of line number nine, Pont de Sèvres-Mairie de Montreuil, beat those of line eight by sixty seconds when everything is running right on time.

From Montreuil, with a morning population of early-rising, blue-collar workers, it takes fifty-nine minutes to reach Boulogne. The population here is still sound asleep at daybreak, worlds away from the early rigors of the night-shifts at the Renault factory, no longer operating today. At Jasmin and La Muette, only a few commuters board the metro. Given how early it is, you'd think they work for a cleaning company. But no one thinks much this early in the day. Along the way, a couple of stations bring to mind the big department stores and the Grands Boulevards. But no one ponders this early in this packed crowd, already belly to belly and back to back, passive, used to all this.

For this mass of humanity, a day unfolds. Right now, no one pays attention to the lessons of urban geography and Parisian history, spelled out in the names of the stations: Abbesses, Pigalle… Concorde, Assemblée Nationale… Hôtel-de-Ville, Saint-Paul, Bastille… Philippe-Auguste, Père-Lachaise… A commuter stifles a yawn, like a tired student, as he awaits the screech of the train on curved tracks, announcing Miromesnil or any station that follows a bend. Not all the trains run straight as does line one, Vincennes-Grande Arche, or the wider, roomier RER trains that link Paris to its suburbs.

The stations file by. They file by quickly on line three-B, the shortest of all: only two stops between Porte des Lilas and Gambetta, Saint-Fargeau and Pelleport. A five-minute commute. Speaking of which, how do you calculate the average commuting time? Optimists multiply the number of stations to travel by a minute and a half, reassuring themselves that you have to be a fool to take your car. The last metro leaves the terminuses at twelve thirty a.m. Do you suppose anyone, at any point during the day, would recall the lyrics of Serge Gainsbourg's popular song, "Le Poinçonneur des Lilas" ("The Lilas Ticket Puncher") before they pass through the automatic gates that no longer close?

SIX A.M.

PRINTED PRESS BY THE BUSHELL

Though Paris sent its printing industry and headquarters of the daily press out to the suburbs, the paper vendors of the Maisons de la Presse (also bookstore clerks), and the kiosk keepers are still very much part of the capital's decor. They represent the last vestiges of trade-on-a-small-scale, once very diversified, perishing today more from the proliferation of office space than from competition with the supermarkets.

The paper vendors get to work at dawn in the early-riser districts, a little later in the affluent districts. They empty shelves and presentation racks of yesterday's unsold copies, making sure to leave *Le Monde* in place for its addicts who never finish it but worry about missing an issue. They put the weeklies and TV guides back in their place, reorganize the kids' press and the theme magazines. Hunting and outdoors, computers, science, do-it-yourself, health and beauty. Expensive magazines on glossy paper, monthlies for twelve francs, weeklies that have changed their format... It all needs to be piled up and packed in, especially when the end-of-the-week supplements arrive, tripling the weight of some dailies. *Le Figaro, Le Parisien, L'Équipe, Libération, Info-Matin, L'Humanité*, all dailies, are delivered in big packets and immediately put in place.

Paper vendors everywhere light their store windows early. They're in the metro and train stations, at street corners, in public squares, at major intersections. The kiosk keepers, often deep-rooted Parisians, are tired of asking for correct change from clients who hand them big bills, tired of being asked the same directions, all day long, in every language. They form their own subculture of hard workers: the shady characters, the funny guys, the quiet ones, the grandpas in caps and the grandmas in knitted jackets. Paper traders, paper prisoners, they know every title and neighborhood client. Some, after a long day of work, don't care to talk; others are able to maintain a small-town *savoir-vivre*...

SIX THIRTY A.M.

OPEN-AIR MARKETS IN EARLY MORNING HOURS

The open-air markets are set up early, especially in low-income neighborhoods and on Sundays when business is good. They're in place early enough to beat the competing small retailers that line the streets, often the same streets. Stallholders, tradesmen of incredible strength and vitality, some traveling long distances with their goods, number nearly two thousand. They share about five thousand plots, some rented for the year, others from time to time, some better located than others, better protected than others... Yearly renters are sometimes heard using the familiar "tu" form with their regular clients, steady traders often look for the spot that previously brought them good business. Then there are the vagabond merchants who wander from one market to another; in a category of their own, they can boast more freedom than their stable counterparts. "Freedom", that is, to work harder at impossible hours.

Set out in colorful displays, where top quality and mediocre sit side by side, fresh produce here is often much better and less expensive than in stores. You do need to compare products, choose, sometimes even bargain with a smile. Behind the displays, the stallholders work non-stop, always ready with a joke, thriving off interaction with clients. Loud-mouthed, they cleverly come up with the appropriate words to hail a client, whether meek and undecided or assertive and sceptical. They unload their merchandize from vans or small isothermal trucks which they sometimes park, backed against the curb, as a reserve supply behind the stall, but often far away. On "big market" days, they arrive while Paris still sleeps and wrap up their goods while Paris lunches... sometimes at the cafeteria or hurriedly grabbing a bite, but that's not the tradesmen's fault.

Some vendors have a warehouse or store, nearby or far away. A few others are local manufacturers or producers. Most of them buy their goods at the national produce market, thirteen kilometers from Paris. Though the largest food distribution center in the world, the Rungis market will never erase from collective memory Les Halles that used to stand in central Paris. Almost as big as the Principality of Monaco, Rungis awakens around midnight, when the first trucks loaded with provisions scan the nondescript warehouses with their headlights. Wagons, carts, fork-lifts spill out from all sides of the warehouses. The first buyers who patronize this ultra-professional market, usually the fishmongers, arrive at around two a.m.; the crowd swells until six. By then, the open-air market folk have already left with their fruit and vegetables, butter, eggs and cheese, poultry, meat and tripe, fish and flowers.

To the right: At 6:30 a.m., on Boulevard Richard-Lenoir, and throughout Paris, market stalls already boast an array of colors.

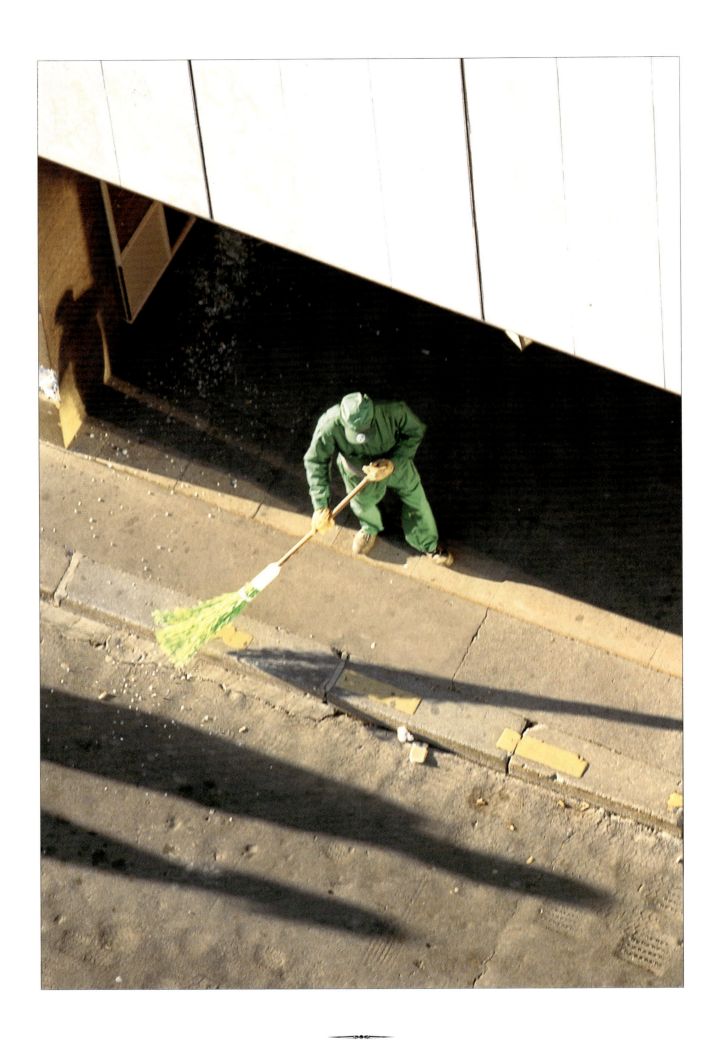

SEVEN A.M.

THE CITY SPRUCES UP

François Mauriac once commented that the street, in Paris, has more significance than the museums. Given Parisians' slovenliness, streets need to be kept clean, not as clean as a street in Geneva, but enough to attract attention. Though it's true that the recently reconditioned Champs-Elysées and some public but prominent squares, streets and gardens receive special treatment, the city's work force does a very decent job of cleaning Paris' 24,000 square kilometers of streets (2,000 kilometers of gutters). About five hundred vehicles, including a battalion of motorcycle poop-scoopers take the offensive: sweepers, sprayers, suckers, arch-cleaners, leaf-blowers, poster-removers. This is not to mention the compression system of the household garbage dumpsters which reduces the volume of collected refuse four or five times…

And in case it should snow? About thirty salters are lined up and ready to go, and nearly as many plows can be mounted on trucks or on sidewalk scooters. Yet the men in green continue to push around their plastic brooms.

17

SEVEN A.M.

ONE ESPRESSO!

The demitasse on the zinc and the hard-boiled egg broken against the counter, made famous by the poet Jacques Prévert, are Parisian artefacts. The coffee is often bad which is why those who know better ask for a cloud of milk to mask the bitterness. The egg is there for show, but at some point, someone will eat it. Someone will absent-mindedly reach for it, trying to remember the words to the poem: "How sad, the sound of the hard-boiled egg broken against the copper counter ..." He'll remember that the poem is harder than the egg, that it's about a very hungry man. He'll recall some phrases: café-crème and hot croissants, hard-boiled egg and café-crème, café laced with rum, two buttered pieces of toast, the waiter's tip... The ending is sad, but that's the poet's prerogative.

Early morning hours in the cafés are not always pleasant, especially on grey, dismal mornings when Paris feels like a suburb, when the suburbs are rushed because Paris works them so hard. And yet, even if you're just passing through, you can find warmth and welcome at the counter. In fact, you'll find more now than later on in the day, except in cafés of Rue des Abbesses and Rue Lepic and in the civilized outskirts. Word has it that Passy and Auteuil soften up at this time of day. Those free-spenders, who come in from elsewhere to work, bring a little humanity from the city fringes to these chic neighborhoods. A sweet gift, though short-lived.

Still, there are those who prefer evening cafés where life and city lights are artificially maintained, where idle clients have all day to chat with nothing to say. It's often particularly hard to find a cozy café during the daytime, at least in the heart of the city.

EIGHT A.M.

SAINT-LAZARE TERMINAL

They arrive from Bécon-les-Bruyères, Asnières, Levallois, Courbevoie as well as from Versailles and Mantes-la-Jolie... The whole western region, inner and outer suburbia, not necessarily more residential than the northern outskirts, floods into the capital. Ten minutes, quarter of an hour, sometimes half an hour commute, dazed with fatigue, in trains crammed full as they approach the end of the line. The Saint-Lazare station links Paris to Deauville for weekend get-aways, to Caen for the weekly business trip, to Normandie for the occasional escapade. But Saint-Lazare is also, and mostly, the "suburban terminal" *par excellence*. Here's where the "suburban trains", often double-deckers, file in from the west. These trains are not to be confused with the RER lines whose colors are more vivid, silhouettes more modern, and who now rival the train service on certain routes where they share the same tracks before interconnecting with the metro network.

A true old-fashioned station with its vast waiting rooms and majestic stairs, the Gare Saint-Lazare does not link directly with the metro as does the Gare du Nord. It's still too traditional to the SNCF, the national train industry. It sits over the intersection of three metro/RER lines and an intricate network of long, underground corridors that do not invite travelers to linger, at least at this time of day. Later on, after lunch, the station's suburban population will be less hurried, less hassled: retired people who come for an afternoon spree in Paris; patrons of the nearby department stores, *Printemps, Galeries Lafayette*; perhaps the well-to-do customers after the *Cartier* jewelry or the *Hermès* scarf at *Fauchon* or *Hédiard*.

Studies estimate that from 130 to 140 million commuters a year, almost every social category represented, use this system. Of these, eighty percent are regulars, day in, day out, year in, year out. Some will cross the Le Havre or Rome courtyard for a lifetime. Will they ever even notice the sculptor Arman's compositions? He piled up clocks to portray "Everyone's Hour" (*L'Heure de tous*) and suitcases to depict "The Lifelong Locker" (*La Consigne à vie*). None of this means much to the hurried commuter, who, suitcase or briefcase in hand, turns around to check the time of the station clocks, making sure that his watch will read the same time as the punch-in clocks.

EIGHT A.M.

Move along!

Today's equivalent of the king's lieutenant and the imperial prefects, the chief of police, or *préfet*, is one of the most powerful figures in Paris, endowed with an unparalleled prerogative to intervene. Everything is his business, whether it be security measures for a foreign leader on official or private visit, supervision of a political demonstration or repression of violent crime. Petty delinquency, parking regulation, traffic flow, public hygiene, supervision of public festivities are also his business. Or rather the State's business. On August 25, 1944, General de Gaulle went first to the prefect headquarters on Ile de la Cité before saluting liberated France at the city hall. There, he honored members of the resistance but also the re-established power of the State.

The prefect headquarters, or *préfecture*, issues drivers licences and vehicle registrations, is responsible for fire prevention, lost and found, supervises taxis, has agents ticket illegally parked cars... Keeping a vigilant eye on the capital, on the lookout for whatever may disturb or disrupt, tracking down those who park anyhow, anywhere, the prefect registers up to 400,000 to 500,000 infringements every year. He rules over 28,000 men and women in uniform and plain-clothes; he can summon up at will national guards and special police forces. Parisians worry about their safety, they worry about muggings and credit card thefts. But their main concern is about cars and about how to avoid traffic jams. Early each morning, police officers in the streets debate about which way to best route traffic. At the same time, a team of technicians works a bit more efficiently, orchestrating the capital's traffic with the aid of computers and screens.

NINE A.M.

The curtain rises on the small retailer

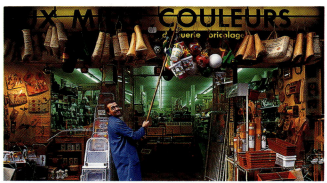

In the outdoor markets, everything is in place; in the bakeries, the first round of baked goods has been sold. Only now do most of the stores open. Paris boasts nearly seven thousand food stores, three or four times the number of other stores, clothing stores coming in second. General stores are dying out, coal merchants have disappeared; on the contrary, ethnic convenience stores and oriental supermarkets are springing up. Everywhere, North Africans sell the essentials: butter, eggs and fresh produce. The vegetables at the corner Vietnamese mini-mart are fresh, from early morning to late night. Drugstores, bookstores are not as plentiful as they once were. There are enough florists and more than enough drycleaners. Likewise, more than enough electronic game stores and perfumeries, which are not to be confused with pharmacies. Though they both vie for customers with an impressive array of beauty products, pharmacies convey their medical vocation with the familiar, blinking lit cross.

Low-income neighborhoods and those with a high percentage of foreigners have been able to preserve their small retailers. These shops contribute to the convivial nature of a big city far more than do austere bank façades. The affluent western sector has also maintained a few streets, lined with small shops, between the Rue de Lévis and Auteuil. They are not as warm as those on the Rue des Abbesses, Rue Dejean, lower Belleville or Rue d'Aligre, but they do give a human dimension to the otherwise introverted neighborhoods.

TEN A.M.

Open the chests!

Everyday, when the murky grey Seine steals a little blue from the sky, especially on wintry Sundays, when the morning walkers bustle by, the *bouquinistes* open their chests. These traders were authorized more than a hundred years ago to leave their wooden cases, all of the same prescribed color and dimensions, on the embankments of the Seine.

The name *bouquiniste*, official since the mid 1700's, came into the language a full century after the word "bouquin", which derives from the Dutch diminutive *boekin*, or little book. And yet the trade itself had been in existence long before the term was defined, only back then, vendors sold not only "second hand" texts but also lampoons and brochures, hailing passers-by as they crossed the just-completed Pont Neuf... Some resorted to selling disparaging pamphlets on a paper that still smelled of fresh ink, resulting in trouble for all of the pedlars. For this and other reasons, they were oftentimes delivered a royal ordinance, chasing the lot of them off bridges and banks.

The *bouquinistes* sell old, not-so-rare books, new books marked down for lack of popularity, whodunits, 1920's paperbacks, science fiction and cartoons, classical and erotic literature, picture books for kids, outdated guides, but also post cards and maps. In short, the *bouquinistes*, whether theme specialists or not, carry everything except the "just come out's". They also sell posters, oft-repeated etchings, and naive little paintings.

Occasionally, a Sunday sketcher or water-color artist works diligently nearby. Will their work, one day, be reproduced in countless lithographs and sold by the *bouquinistes*, just like that of their impressionist ancestors? Not very likely. Better to count on finding among the books tucked tightly into the big chests which poet compared the Seine to the arms of a lovely blond, for the duration of a short rhyme (Aragon, *Il ne m'est Paris que d'Elsa*)...

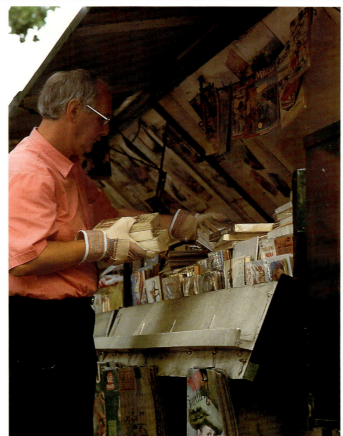

There aren't many morning walkers out when the bouquinists open their chests. These boxes hold a variety of volumes: books that once lay on bedside tables, humble printed treasures, earlier popular magazines.

TEN A.M.

THE FLOWERED COBBLESTONES

Approximately two thousand florists supply Paris and its outskirts with the seasons' colors, the scents of remote regions of France and blossoms from afar. Bringing incessantly renewed polychromatic colors to the grey streets, they exhilarate neighborhoods unfamiliar with the orchid, they remedy with their magic the elegant boredom of bourgeois districts where hidden terraces are more flower-adorned than street windows.

This morning, a store framed in green, its quaint sobriety perfectly in tune with the elegant Place du Palais-Bourbon, has its terraces decked in a fresh floral display. The sidewalk is not yet in full bloom, but Moulié's shop has been open for two hours. One can step into a different world here, among the colorful displays, charming and thoughtfully composed, not in the least pretentious. This store, moderate in size, has occupied for the last fifteen years the ground-floor of a mansion that once belonged to the family of Charles Percier, one of Napoleon's favored architects. The Mouliés are masters in coordinating flowers from the immediate area, from the Côte d'Azur, from Israel and from other horticultural countries. The displays are monochromatic or tone on tone, matched delicately or radiantly. There's no room here for *nouveau riche* exuberance nor pretentious parsimony, but only for tasteful delicacy and zingy freshness.

The left bank boasts numerous florists, some of them very sophisticated. On the right bank, Parisians casually buy their flowers at *Primfleurs* on Avenue de Villiers, at *Nice Fleurs*, or in one of the *Monceau Fleurs*, an inexpensive chain store. One can spend up to ten times more on flowers elsewhere. *Lachaume*, located in the 8th arrondissement, has been around for more than a century. Is this the capital's most renowned florist? The owner, a noted professional, certainly ranks among the most expensive, but he continues to sell the "cattleya" (the rare orchid that Marcel Proust used to buy to adorn his lapel), floral compositions of ultimate perfection, and exquisite bouquets of roses. We are near *Maxim's* here, where decorators, trained in the *École de Nancy*, painted winding chains of stylized flowers. The name of the once fashionable restaurant now serves as a label on items in *Maxim's* store, imitation 1900 style, where one can buy orchids and *fleurs de lys* in luxurious vases, each lavishly outclassing the other...

TEN FIFTEEN A.M.

Fresh endives here!

One can capture Paris' true flavor in streets where shop windows, stalls and displays abound. Central and residential districts have lost their small retailers and seasonal traders, but shopper's dreamlands have survived here and there, even in the posh 16th arrondissement. Twice a week, the little Place Charles-Lorrain takes on airs of a small village; the outdoor market in Auteuil gives the Rue de l'Annonciation a joyous atmosphere every morning. As residents of central Paris shop on the colorful Rue Montorgueil, they fondly remember the warmth and hardiness of Les Halles, transferred to Rungis in the early seventies. Small cafés move over to make place for hip bars, but the street has a great flavor in the morning hours and the neighborhood a younger look since its recent improvements. The 17th, though dismal in places, has maintained two shopper-streets: Rue Poncelet, now a pedestrian street, and especially the captivating Rue de Lévis, partially cleared of cars and today a customer's paradise. Fruit and vegetables sit alongside one another in gorgeous presentations; one can buy fine meats, tasty cold cuts and perfectly matured cheese.

In this category, the 18th is a particularly spoiled arrondissement with the Rue Lepic and Rue des Abbesses, boasting the huge Barbès market, sheltered underneath the aerial metro line. We find here the brightly colored, exotic streets of the Goutte d'Or, today home to ethnic populations from Africa and the West Indies, as well as the Rue Dejean with La Chapelle's lovely covered market. The Belleville residents shop at their spacious sidewalk markets where ethnic accents prevail. Bastille shoppers hesitate between Boulevard Richard-Lenoir and the Aligre quarter. Impossible on this one page to do justice to all the capital's worthy stalls! So, rendez-vous on the left bank. Situated at the intersection of Boulevard Saint-German and Rue Monge, the little Maubert esplanade bustles on Saturday mornings. The well-known Rue Mouffetard descends gently towards Saint-Médard, whetting appetites along the way. The Monge market, Rue de Seine and Rue de Buci, Rue Cler are classic shopper's havens. Colors mix with convivial tones. The Raspail market isn't bad either, but Sunday mornings devoted to the anti-chemical fanatics have become hip and snobby.

Paris, or rather the City Hall, has prohibited the implantation of supermarkets. Housewives make do - quite well, in fact - by shopping at pleasant, colorful, and lively open-air markets. Some may choose one of the few covered markets, often in structures of fine architecture, but where some stalls lack color and charm. These outdoor markets accommodate year-round traders, from dawn to one p.m., two or three times a week, as well as sporadic stall-holders who may or may not set up, depending on the season, available space and the weather. Customers find everything in these markets, essentially food products, but also household items, crockery, clothes. Some traders sell flowers, freshly delivered from southern France or Holland, different kinds of honey and baked goods that send us back to our childhood.

ELEVEN A.M.

THE REPUBLICAN GUARD

The colossal Célestins barracks, stretching its lengthy façade on Boulevard Henri-IV, has been the headquarters of the Republican Guard since the late 19th century. Founded in 1802 to bestow honors on the State's highest authorities as well as on foreign leaders, this section of the police force is also in charge of the security of national edifices. The enormous structure, situated near the severe Arsenal converted into a library, is home for seven hundred men... and five hundred and twenty-three horses. Here, boarding police-officers of the Cavalry Brass Band *(Fanfare de Cavalerie)* rehearse with members of the Guard Orchestras *(Orchestres de la Garde)*. This team is not to be confused with the Musique de la Garde, located on Boulevard Kellermann...

The Célestins barracks is the cavalrymen's private kingdom, similar to the Carnot district behind the Vincennes fort and the barracks in Saint-Germain-en-Laye. Approximately twenty other barracks, reserved for the infantrymen, dot the capital. The Republican Guard also has two infantry regiments. In theory, the policemen always mount and care for the same horse. Though two blacksmiths remain on site at their disposal, there are no grooms at the Boulevard Henri-IV barracks.

Parisians are used to seeing, and sometime hearing, the Guard cavalry parade through the streets. An open house, usually held on the second weekend of June, provides an occasion for civilians to learn about this grand institution. One can also attend demonstrations organized once a month by requesting an invitation.

Built in "Louis XIII-neo florentine" style, the barracks were erected on the gardens of the large estate belonging to the Célestin monks. Their sumptuous convent stood on what are today the even numbers of the Rue du Petit-Musc, a medieval artery drawn long before the Marais district was systematically divided up. The monastery monuments that abutted a lovely *Renaissance* cloister were rebuilt around 1730 and, in 1904, turned over to demolition contractors. Nothing stands either of the monastery church, noted for the precious funeral relics that it sheltered. Those that encased the hearts of Henri II and Anne de Montmorency are currently at the Louvre.

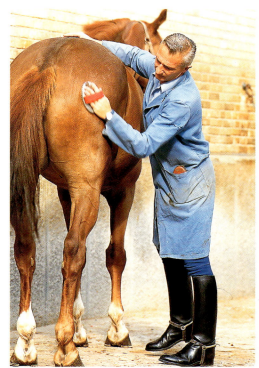

ELEVEN A.M.
THE ROSES OF BAGATELLE

Bagatelle, from the Italian word *bagatella*, literally means "juggler's trick", but can be translated as "whim"... The lovely miniature chateau, erected in record-breaking time for the young comte d'Artois, was the setting for many gallant rendez-vous and furtive kisses. The future Charles X, brother of Louis XVI and Louis XVIII who, history says, was most intolerant, indulged there in fervent merrymaking with decadent company. In the 19th century, some British landowners bought the estate, among them Richard Wallace who had donated the Parisian fountains. As true Englishmen, devoted to gardens, they enlarged the park and rearranged the terraces. In order to prevent the property from being divided up into plots, the city of Paris acquired it in 1905. Today, this fifty-nine acre parcel, enclosed within the Bois de Boulogne, is a municipal garden open to the public.

The city's Parks and Gardens Service takes particularly good care of the Bagatelle. More than four thousand employees work for this service, manicuring the woods, squares, walkways, and literally hundreds of resting spots and floral decorations throughout the capital. At the Bagatelle, nearly forty gardeners clip hedges, pamper buds until they explode into the colors and scents of the famous rose garden, orchestrate the blossoming of flowers that reflect the season: crocuses in February, tulips from March to May, peonies in May, irises and clematis in May and June, roses in June and July, camellias in November and December... This vast enclosure from which one can view the skyscrapers of the Défense, is the most captivating of all public parks and gardens.

ELEVEN FIFTEEN A.M.

Employees lunch at the *Ambassade d'Auvergne*

At the dawn of 1995, a team of well-known chefs, among them Marc Menau and Marc Haeberlin, along with France's top culinary columnists, some gourmet foreign journalists (two Japanese) and a few scholarly connoisseurs founded a culinary club, *"Saveurs de France"*. This informal group of hard-core professionals, casual yet earnest, assembled a wide variety of Parisian restaurateurs: from Jean Laurent (*Fermette Marbeuf 1900)* to the Vifian brothers (*Tan Dinh* where you eat with chopsticks while sipping the best of French wines). The club's hastily composed jury awarded without hesitation the prize for best regional menu in Paris to *L'Ambassade d'Auvergne*. A unanimous vote.

Above, a picture of the winning team, just after eleven o'clock, when the employees sit down for lunch. One does a better job of waiting tables on a full stomach. Today, they have chosen to eat at the ground floor table. The sort of table where you feel invited to take in the *plat du jour* (daily specials), to peruse the menu, to exchange greetings with those at neighboring tables, to be charmed by the attractive head waiter.

The owner, Françoise Moulier, is a hard working woman who acquired the family enterprise, located near the Pompidou Center. With a reputation dating back twenty-five years, *L'Ambassade d'Auvergne* ranks among the steady, traditional restaurants that draw their cuisine from a certain province or country. These regional restaurants are now few and far between in the capital; we can mention with pride *Le Trou gascon, Benoît, Le Restaurant du Marché, Moisonnier, Le Grizzly, Lous Bascou, L'Alsaco* and *Lous Landès*, also recognized by the jury for its *cassoulet*, a popular haricot bean dish from the Toulouse area. In the kitchen of these restaurants, cooks respectfully prepare and renew grand-mother's recipes, specialities that whet appetites, that satisfy hungers yet don't send us home broke. At *L'Ambassade*, you may be served the traditional, simple slice of ham, or better still, *aligot* (a thick, cheese *purée*), stuffed cabbage, *andouillette* labelled AAAAA (the best there is), white sausage with chestnuts, cheese from the Massif Central mountains. All this accompanied by a wide variety of exquisite wines from Pétillat, Lapouge, Viguier, Valady... In short, *L'Ambassade* speaks to us of a particular region.

NOON
AT THE POMPIDOU CENTER

It's almost noon; the Georges-Pompidou Center is about to open its doors to the public. The first wave of visitors includes those who won't bother to visit the Museum of Modern Art or any of the exhibition halls, but also those regularly drawn to the casual atmosphere of the BPI, Library of Public Information. Offering the public a wide range of publications, recent books as well as classics, this is a pleasant spot to take time out. That is, if you can find a seat, which isn't always the case when students, teachers, researchers, specialists, browsers, cartoon buffs, and others assemble. The eye-catching structure, designed by Rogers and Piano, that houses the polycultural center President Pompidou dreamed of (still called "Beaubourg" by its regulars), ranks among Paris' most visited monuments along with the Louvre, the Eiffel Tower and Notre-Dame.

The National Center for Art and Culture, to use its full name, is a civilized showcase, open to scholars, loafers, tourists, amateurs of *avant-garde* art, to everyone. Though some are happy simply to take the free ride up the panoramic escalator, others don't know which way to turn: read, observe, listen, dawdle, chat? Here, people either switch from one culture to another or delve into one in depth. Thousands of books stand at the public's disposal to understand, learn and escape: newspapers and periodicals, music of today and tomorrow, foreign films from other eras, contemporary design, activities for children, works of Matisse, Picasso, Picabia, Ernst, Ben. This extraordinary laboratory, twenty years after its opening, continues to promote activities as diverse as research, esthetic contemplation and mindless wandering.

Popularity has taken its toll on the eight-storey metal and glass structure. The surroundings need improvements, and construction work is expected to last until the year 2000. The doors, nonetheless, will remain open to this once highly controversial edifice, today almost unanimously accepted, just like the Louvre Pyramid.

TWELVE THIRTY P.M.

To see and be seen at the *Café de Flore*

Would Boris Vian, who knew everything about Saint-Germain-des-Prés, have dared read Roland Barthes at the terrace of *Café de Flore*? He would have undoubtedly shown interest in the reader at the table nearby, offered her other mythological tales. The *Flore* of those days earned its legendary fame from "Prévert's gang", mixing ill-assorted intellectuals, united by their quick minds, humor, flair for puns and the latest joke. Among them Marcel Duhamel, Maurice Baquet, Raymond Bussières, Roger Blin, the young Mouloudji... The *Flore*'s first regulars were all successful in their respective fields, recognized scholars. Before the Second World War, the café's terrace looked as it does today, probably with more aura and conviviality. (As one regular wrote, "Upon our return from travels, our first outing took us to the *Flore* for cocktails. Of the two hundred hands present, there were one hundred eighty to shake.") The illustrious Boubal, who took on the *Flore* in 1939, hosted a wide variety of patrons: André Breton, Tristan Tzara, Trauner, but also trendy journalists, several of them American, colorful characters, good-looking women, some smart, some agreeably dense.

The *Flore*, more or less heated (at least it was warmer than the *Dôme*), reinforced its clientele loyalty during the dark hours of the occupation. Sartre started as a regular in 1942 with Simone de Beauvoir, spending entire days there. As Boubal recalls, "He often came with a woman; they'd sit distanced from one another at different tables." Sartre, who stopped coming when his admirers became numerous and invasive, spoke of the *Flore* with affection: "It was like an English club. People would come in, everyone knew everyone else, knew the finest details of his neighbor's private life. But from one table to another, we didn't exchange greetings. And yet should we happen to meet elsewhere, we'd salute each other warmly..."

The *Flore* assembled young authors, *Les Deux Magots* the old literary scholars and *Lipp*, the political buffs. Everyone patronized *La Rhumerie Martiniquaise*, everyone except the intellectuals and their likes who complained of the noise. The clientele moved downstairs when the jazz-club era began (*Le Tabou, Le Méphisto, Le Club Saint-Germain-des-Prés, Le Vieux Colombier* where Claude Luter played, *La Rose Rouge*). They resurfaced to plunge again, first at *Régine's, Castel,* then at the *King Club* which continues to operate, always undergoing redecoration. The pure-bred locals started to dissipate around the seventies, but respectable bourgeois, out for an evening, and the young crowd, have succeeded them. They all keep reasonable hours, except on Saturdays; after all, people work now, and money is harder to come by, say even those who have it. The *Flore* (on right), has maintained its cult; *Les Deux Magots* and *Lipp* are also still around.

ONE P.M.

THE GRÉVIN MUSEUM OPENS ITS DOORS

Alfred Grévin (1827-1872) was a skilled caricaturist. The Parisians loved his best-seller album, *Les Parisiennes,* and faithfully followed his sketches in the *Journal Amusant.* But his name rings familiar today because of the wax museum he founded in 1882 where once stood a café. Among the most visited museums of Paris, both stylishly old-fashioned and contemporary, set in gold and marble decor, Grévin enchants his public with the sound, light and magic shows of the *Palais des Mirages* and the fantasy room.

The Grévin Museum on Boulevard Montmartre (there is a second one at the Forum des Halles, very *Belle Époque)* opens its doors earlier during school holidays, but the dummies' normal workday runs from one to seven p.m. The wax figures in the basement are certified and belong to ranks of both great and petty history. They will remain there. Those on the ground floor are today's stars. Their selection is based on fashion, the political scene, television's whims and the ascension of media-borne personalities. Mr. Biby, one of the museum's keepers for the past fifteen years, has been "statufied", a true claim to fame... but he doesn't worry about joining the ranks of wax heroes. A few minutes of total immobility, and then he gives a hint of a movement... Thanks, Mr. Biby, for the startling trick that works every time!

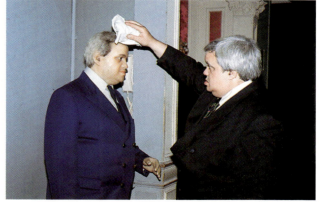

Monsieur Biby is in good company. Whether with Michael Jackson or facing himself, he knows, in all circumstances, how to keep his cool.

Alain Dutournier, in the kitchen of *Carré des Feuillants*. A chef with a mind of his own, he didn't wait for the recent "rural flavor fad" to demonstrate his ties with the south-western region of France. He made a name for himself in the mid 1970's at the *Trou Gascon*, now managed by his wife, Nicole.

ONE THIRTY P.M.

DUTOURNIER IN THE KITCHEN

Many Parisians will contend that any true gourmet is from the capital. Though provincial gourmets can justifiably argue that Paris does not hold the monopoly on fine *cuisine*, the capital does offer a variety of marvelous restaurants where one can count on eating well, usually very well. Choices abound, especially on the right bank. The only condition to divine eating is being able to afford it, and, of course, having adventurous taste buds.

Gault-Millau, two Parisian culinary columnists, worked hard to promote the idea of *nouvelle cuisine*. Though some claim the movement originated in Paris, Alain Chapel influenced trends in Mionnay, and Bocuse shopped for his produce in Lyon... Today, people speak of it as snobby and mannered, but, in a revolutionary fashion, it brought about the return to simpler tastes, discreetly magnified. Around 1970, Parisians put aside intricate recipes and complicated sauces to rediscover the "real taste" of foods and find pride in just the right cooking time, playing around, paradoxically, with suggested eccentricities. Through time, things changed, and helpings grew bigger. We laugh today at menu entries like "filleted feather", once so popular. Now we want strong tastes, laced with rural savors... just what the advocates of *nouvelle cuisine* prescribed but in different terms. A sign of the times: a gourmet club crowned Alain Dutournier, acclaimed for having preserved the culinary accent of his province in spite of twenty years of Parisian *brio*.

ONE FORTY-FIVE P.M.

EXQUISITE MENUS AND DAILY SPECIALS

Since the mid 1980's, Joël Robuchon has drawn recognition for his meticulous professionalism, his implacable rigor and his complete mastery in new situations. From superlative to overstatement, he is today Robuchon The Great, Robuchon The Wealthy. He has never let his kitchen team ruin one of his carefully thought-out dishes. Every meal at his restaurant is truly memorable. A certified chef of the century, Robuchon will be a name remembered in the history of gastronomy. He reigns in his sumptuous new restaurant, patronizing an elite clientele. Word has it that he will soon step back from the pressures of the profession.

Let's have a look at Robuchon's itinerary, that of a typical Parisian chef. Born and raised in the provinces, as were all the great cooks starred by Michelin, his entire career has unfolded in the capital. He started out in a restaurant on Ile de la Cité, worked at the *Berkeley*, then the former *Frantel Rungis*, *Concorde-Lafayette*, *Nikko* and *Jamin*, on the Rue de Longchamp. Would he affirm Parisian supremacy in the culinary domain?

"Many chefs from the provinces are exemplary", he remarked in 1994 when he took over the premises on Avenue Raymond-Poincaré. "In their style, their trade, their approach, their strong personality... But all levels considered, Paris has more to offer than the rest of France. One can find all types of cooking, excellent produce, and customer potential significant enough for successful business."

Paris once had Les Halles, today has Rungis, and has always had direct deliveries. The capital draws talented chefs from the provinces, in exchange for little more than an occasional culinary novelty that slowly dies in the rural reaches. Of the big chefs who started their career in Paris, only one returned to the provinces: Michel Guérard, already well known when he left Paris, came into fame in the tiny Tursan area, known only to geographers and the Aquitain residents.

As Balzac and Zola's writings underline, Paris has always had a drawing force. Most *brasserie* managers are originally from Auvergne, Aveyron, or Alsace. René Lasserre came north from Bayonne, Raymond Oliver was from Langon, Alain Senderens, from the Pyrénées, has preserved a slight south-western accent. Alain Dutournier is a native of Cagnotte in Chalosse, Guy Savoy is from Dauphine, Alain Passard from Bretagne. Christian Constant, head of the kitchens of the famous *Grillon*, comes from the Midi Pyrénées region. Guy Martin, chef at *Le Grand Véfour*, which for years was the orphan of Raymond Olivier, is Savoyard. Ghislaine Arabian, who plays lovely music with Flemish tonalities at *Ledoyen*, claims to be a northerner.

Paris picks the savors of France's gardens so that provincial chefs can enhance them for the benefit of a clientele that is both provincial and foreign. But is there a Parisian dish? Maybe the steak & French-fries served in the *café-restaurants*.

There's really nothing to add about Joël Robuchon, already heralded by the media (above left). A few words though on Guy Savoy (above right), a talented, creative forty-year-old with a fighting spirit. Already quite well known, he continues to prosper in his lovely, ultra-contemporary restaurant of the Rue Troyon. Robuchon, Savoy: contemporary gastronomic history in motion.

Opposite, René Chartier, the father, and Daniel Chartier, the son, sitting down to eat... at the Chartier's. We are at the heart of Parisian history. The *Bouillon Chartier* at 7 Rue du Faubourg-Montmartre, dates back to 1898. The decor is most inviting: a tinted glass roof, framed in a light frieze, little numbered cubby-holes for the napkins, impressive and immense dining rooms. One can eat here for less than a hundred francs: hard-boiled egg with mayonnaise, veal stew, caramel custard. The gamut of restaurants in Paris can please any palate.

TWO P.M.

LAZING IN THE PUBLIC GARDEN

Under the Old Regime, the upper crust and, for the occasional open house, the common people, would visit the Tuileries, the Luxembourg, the Jardin des Plantes, the Jardin du Palais-Royal and the Bagatelle. The Second Empire added the two vast wooded areas and the three big parks that honor the capital with their greenery (Bois de Boulogne, Bois de Vincennes, Monceau, Buttes-Chaumont, Montsouris) and approximately twenty additional public gardens. Among them, the Square Louvois, inaugurated in 1859 in honor of Napoléon III. This is not to mention the improvements of the Jardin des Champs-Elysées by Alphand, brilliant planner of the capital's green zones. During the years between the wars, Paris acquired pleasant public gardens and the Parc de la Butte-du-Chapeau-Rouge, built on the old fortifications. The city has recently been further endowed with new spots to relax, play, and dream, owing mostly to the initiative of Jacqueline Nebout, deputy mayor in charge of the Environment, Parks, Gardens and Green Zones. The State contributed the Parc de la Villette, a fabulous play space, conceived with talent and audacity, and financed the long overdue renovation of the Tuileries-Carrousel ensemble.

Many Parisians love the old public gardens and their likes. They offer benches for a stolen nap or useless chatter before heading back to the office, a little bit of sand, maybe a tired climbing structure; there is a sense of peace and quiet behind the swinging green gates. But the city gardeners offer us far better than this.

Parisians recently acquired two parks at the capital's extremities, orchestrated with an entirely original view, based finally on contemporary architecture, intriguing and pleasant to the eye. To the west, the Parc André Citroën features sophisticated architecture with its thematic gardens, greenhouses, computerized fountains and an area of untouched woodlands. It brightens up the banks of the Seine which, here, are somewhat insipid. To the east, well hidden, the Coulée Verte (green flow) follows the route of the old train tracks, while the Parc de Bercy grows in size and originality. Things have also happened in the 13th, 14th and 18th arrondissements; a miniature garden will appear here and there, often astutely defying city planning.

TWO P.M.

LIBRARIES AND *LE MONDE*

At about this time of day, it's hard to find a place to sit at the Sainte-Geneviève Library. The reading hall, an iron and steel structure, seats approximately 750 students. The immense, imposing building, located Place du Panthéon, is the work of Henri Labrouste who later designed the reading hall of the *Bibliothèque nationale*. A true pioneer of metal architecture, he supervised construction of the Sainte-Geneviève Library from 1844 to 1850.

The library houses nearly 2,700,000 volumes and, in the reserve collection, a quantity of treasures: exquisite bindings from different eras, manuscripts of Baudelaire, Rimbaud, Verlaine, Mallarmé, Gide, Valéry, Mauriac, Breton... Erected to shelter the illuminated parchments and early printed books of the ancient abbey of Sainte-Geneviève (today *Lycée Henri-IV*), the library stands where the famous but ignominious Montaigu School once was. Ignace de Loyola, Erasme and Calvin studied humanities there before the Revolution closed the school. Undernourished, dirty, made to rise at four and work almost non-stop until nine, the students were severely punished by harsh, whip-brandishing fathers... Rabelais, who probably studied there, regarded it as "a miserable, wretched school"; yet the quality of the education one acquired was said to be excellent.

The daily newspaper, *Le Monde*, a spirited fifty-year-old, gave its presentation a face-lift in early 1995. The editorial offices, moved in 1990 into a high-tech structure on Rue Falguière, are linked with the printing facilities in Ivry via a highly sophisticated system, allowing for transmission of fully mounted pages. The last draft, called the *Une*, full page of the latest news, leaves Montparnasse before noon; the headquarters may transmit updates as late as mid-afternoon. The Wyfag presses start rolling at around noon, and the first edition comes out at one o'clock sharp. Shipments to the provinces are immediately sent out via plane or TGV trains (several of the bigger cities receive, that same evening, the paper dated for the next day). Only an hour later, approximately 200,000 copies will already have come off the press... By then, the major distribution points in the capital have received their orders.

The parcels of newspapers are loaded into minivans or carried off by motorcyclists and delivered to vendors and kiosk keepers in early afternoon (delivery to the suburbs is a little later). *Le Monde*'s advanced technology allows for last minute updates, until around two thirty, insuring that the kiosks have the daily by four. This schedule could probably suffer a further setback, should something earthshattering occur...

51

THREE P.M.

THE LORD'S TERRITORY

Paris has close to two hundred catholic communities spread throughout the twenty arrondissements: a hundred and fifty for women, fifty for men. Celibate Catholics, the men and women who have opted for religious life and the rigorous practice of evangelic counsel, have not necessarily taken vows, but they nonetheless adhere to the strict regulations of their communities. Some preach, others teach, care for the ill or tend to those in need...

Everyone knows or claims to know les Petites Sœurs des Pauvres, les Filles de la Charité, les Oratoriens, les Frères des Écoles Chrétiennes, the priests who live in clerical congregations, like the Pères Marist and the Assomptionnistes. What everyone may not know is that Carmelites live in the shadows of Sacré-Cœur, on Rue du Chevalier-de-la-Barre, that a community of Clarisses lives on Villa de Saxe in the 7th arrondissement, that the 14th arrondissement hosts Franciscan men and women, Sœurs de Saint-Joseph-de-Cluny, and Sœurs de la Visitation Sainte-Marie... On Rue Lecourbe, hospitallers of Saint-Jean-de-Dieu care for disabled children. On Rue de l'Assomption, the nuns ... of the Assumption organize four-day retreats before Christmas and Easter. On Rue du Bac, one can visit the Asian library and the Foreign Missions' "hall of martyrs". Further along the same street, les Filles de la Charité de Saint-Vincent-de-Paul keep watch over the chapel of the Médaille Miraculeuse, where the virgin appeared to Catherine Labouré. Their convent, which includes the beautiful residence of La Vallière, given by the city in 1815, had until recently the distinguished honor of housing the remains of Vincent de Paul, referred to as "Mr. Vincent". The precious relics of the "great saint of the Great Century" were transferred to Rue de Sèvres, to the Lazarist's chapel, where pilgrims flock to meditate before the shrine.

The various religious congregations in the capital today own close to two hundred acres. Some raise fruit and vegetables, others make their own honey. Couldn't we think of Paris as a little corner of paradise?

THREE FIFTEEN P.M.

ALONG THE CANAL

Nine locks for a stretch that measures less than five kilometers... The Canal Saint-Martin, very Parisian, charms the 10th arrondissement before it slips underground. It flows under the new gardens and bustling market of Boulevard Richard-Lenoir, before reaching Place de la Bastille. (The *Génie*, gold statue perched atop the Bastille monument, ready to take wing, seems to ignore the canal as it arrives in the Arsenal Basin, reconstructed as a pleasure port.) An extension of the Canal Saint-Denis and the Canal de l'Ourcq, it sometimes pushes along a shallow-draft barge (we are worlds away from the enormous convoys proper to today's inland water transport). Many tourist ferries and panoramic flatboats drift under the canal's pretty metal footbridges, sometimes taking on Venetian airs. (The Douane footbridge, known for its extraordinary delicacy, situated near the Rue Léon-Jouhaux, dates back to 1860). It's hard to believe that in 1960, some dared to suggest building a wide waterway in place of this *canal d'opérette*, dug from 1802 to 1825 to relieve the Seine of its rapidly growing traffic.

The quiet ribbon of water reflects the *Hôtel du Nord*, made legendary by both the author, Eugène Dabit (the owners' son), and the film writer, Marcel Carné. The edifice, fortunately, has been preserved; its façade remained standing during reconstruction. Most of the spacious workshops, however, which faced the river walkways, have given way to contemporary apartment complexes... none of which speak in favor of today's architecture.

THREE THIRTY P.M.

CHECKMATE AT LUXEMBOURG

Owned by the Senate which sits in the "Florentine Palace" (built by Salomon de Brosse on request of Catherine de Médicis), the Luxembourg Garden is named after a mansion she bought in 1612. This double-terraced garden with majestic walkways, 224,000 square meters abutting the Latin Quarter, looks very much today as it did in 1625, when Henri IV's widow settled in, preferring this estate over the Louvre. The major difference today is the beautiful, open perspective from the palace which, earlier, was marred by the high wall of a convent.

The garden, opened to the public in the 17th century (with an entrance fee under Louis XVI), is the capital's most visited; all ages, social categories, and types mingle here. Students flock to dream in the sun or study their notes; lovers forget that they're not alone; kids relish in the numerous activities at their disposal: a play space for toddlers, sandboxes, a merry-go-round, swings, pony-rides and a puppet theater. The chess addicts, like the bowl players, have their reserved areas. They retreat to the quiet spots where foul balls can't knock over a king, queen, or pawn... The Garden offers leisure activities so varied as to include real-tennis, croquet and courses in apiculture.

Diderot, Baudelaire, Hugo and Sainte-Beuve walked among the garden's 3,500 trees, some remarkable in their size, age and rarity: the enlightened amateurs all know the copper beech tree that towers in the fruit garden, standing near the Judea tree, the Chinese cedar, the silver birch, the giant sequoia and the Caucase elm (inventory limited to the stretch bordering Rue Auguste-Comte!). Loved by Watteau, described by Lamartine as a "solitary refuge, yet open dawn to dusk", the Luxembourg has attracted writers throughout the centuries. André Gide evoked the vendor stalls in *Si le grain ne meurt*, and Hemingway would idle here on his way from the *Coupole* to the *Closerie des Lilas*.

FOUR P.M.

LE GRAND LOUVRE

At his first press conference as President of the French Republic, François Mitterrand voiced his commitment to "bring the Louvre to its destination." Two presidential terms later, the archaic palace of abundant riches, previously impractical and congested with ministerial offices, has finally become *le Grand Louvre*. Today it is a stupendous monument-museum, for which the glass pyramid, at first so controversial, has become the symbol.

A series of inaugurations have taken place in the last few years. The first opened the famous pyramid in the Cour Napoléon, leading to an underground labyrinth, prodigiously planned by Ieoh Ming Pei. In 1993, two hundred years after the opening of the Muséum Central des Arts, in which the *Jaconde* (Mona Lise) held a place of honor, the president inaugurated the Richelieu wing. This impressive addition features three covered courtyards, 165 rooms, an escalator designed by Pei, works of art, displayed and presented by Wilmotte. Twelve thousand paintings that had been cleaned and restored were superbly placed for viewing, a throng of sculptures delicately draped in daylight (fine work of the architect Michel Macary)... The Richelieu wing also houses the treasure of Saint-Denis, the twelve tapestries of the Chasses de Maximilien, French paintings from the 15th to early 17th centuries, paintings from Holland, Flanders, Germany... The guards, men and women, appear younger and friendlier from one day to the next. There are two cafés with elegant yet astute decor, information desks here and there... In short, a most successful transformation. It's hard to believe that the finance ministers kept such a firm hold on these premises from 1871 to 1989. The VIP's were forced out against their will, most reluctant to resettle in the new, modern offices of Bercy.

A third inauguration took place in late 1994, to open the rooms of the Denon wing, masterfully rearranged by Catherine Bizouard and François Pin, who, at times, grappled fiercely with the old structure. This wing gave a new look to Italian, Spanish and Scandinavian sculptors. Now we await the dawn of 1996 to rediscover the Egyptian collections.

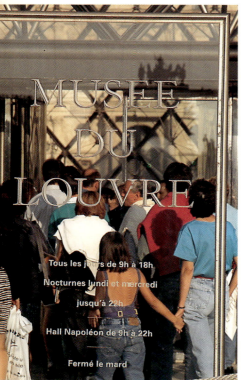

FOUR FIFTEEN P.M.

NOTRE-DAME AND HER ARTISTS

Beginning near 1160 and for three centuries thereafter, Notre-Dame de Paris, "the parish of France's history", was the work of a succession of both anonymous builders and glorified architects of French history (Jean de Chelles, Pierre de Montreuil, Jean Ravy). Neglected and partially ruined in the 18th century, ransacked during the Revolution, Victor Hugo fortunately brought it back to public attention when it had reached a pitiful state of dilapidation. Restored by Viollet-le-Duc, the cathedral was then rediscovered by a generation suddenly impassioned by gothic architecture, for years discredited or unknown. It only then reclaimed its title of the queen of Paris. Today, Notre-Dame is a besieged monument, a tourists' hunting-ground, proudly displaying new colors since its face-lift, most of which was finished in 1995.

Notre-Dame has always attracted painters. The *promenades* of the left bank offer a wide choice of angles: the façade, backing off to the Petit-Pont for a proper perspective; the southern flank, from the Pont-au-Double; the *chevet*, from the Pont de l'Archevêché, or perhaps from the very end of the Pont Saint-Louis. The artist can also frame the cathedral between two *bouquiniste* chests, or add some greenery... The panoramic flatboats seldom appear on these paintings; these vessels with their abrupt lines are far less inspiring than the fishing dories and paddle boats that Jongkind depicted, or the barges of Marquet's times. Furthermore, they lack the picturesque quality of the river craft that fascinated illustrators back when river banks, bare and shapeless or settled and colorful, teemed with a laboring life-style. Many painters of the time matter-of factly reported daily life around them.

FOUR THIRTY P.M.

WAIT FOR ME AT THE GATE!

Long before the 16th century, Paris was an established city of scholars. Parisians were proud of their university that had originated in ascetic and sparse conditions in the Notre-Dame cloister, before expanding and moving to the left bank in 12th century. Let's not forget that the name *Quartier latin* originates from the official language of academics under the Ancient Regime. Louis XI designated Saint-Charlemagne day, the 28th of January, as a holiday for the *Sorbonne*. François I, Guillaume Budé and twelve royal lecturers created a new form of education in 1530 with the *Collège des Trois Langues* (School of the Three Languages), the future *Collège de France*, in which Latin, Greek and Hebrew were taught. Today, more than 360,000 students (nearly 215,000 in Paris proper) are enrolled in the seventeen universities of greater Paris, which cover all disciplines. The system has been decentralized for close to twenty years (regional campuses include Orsay, Nanterre, Saint-Denis, Châtenay-Malabry...), but many students would rather study in the capital, at the *Sorbonne, Dauphine, Assas, Tolbiac* or *Jussieu...*

It all starts in nursery school: Paris accommodates 60,000 youngsters in the public schools, a third that many in private schools. One hundred thousand students attend elementary schools, most of them public. Policewomen stand diligently by the gates at this time everyday, supervising the exodus. The youthful glee of this daily parade brightens up the street for as long as it takes this young population to walk home or retreat to the *concierge*'s until Mom gets home from work. Then comes adolescence: nearly 100 middle schools *(collèges)* and 130 high schools *(lycées)*, unevenly dispersed, open their doors to this pre-Baccalaureate generation. Private schools boast high enrollment in the secondary level (counting more than a third of Paris' young population), but these figures decrease for the demanding preparatory schools. Here, the public institutions have higher ratings, with *Lycée Henri-IV* in the lead.

Parisian parents embark on a mad scramble, as soon as their child reaches age, to ensure enrollment in one of the top middle schools, guaranteeing high grades on the Baccalaureate exam and acceptance into one of France's reputable universities, the *grandes écoles*. Every strategy is employed (choosing an obscure language, faking an address in order to fall within the coveted school district) to gain acceptance at *Louis-le-Grand, Saint-Louis, Chaptal* or *Fénelon*. And yet Paris has some fine private institutions, known for their high percentage of awarded Baccalaureates: l'*École Alsacienne*, for example, or *"Stan" (Stanislas)*, the Jesuit school, reconstructed in the sixties.

FIVE P.M.

AT THE ZOO

At the edge of the Bois de Vincennes, near the artificial Lac Daumesnil, the zoological park projects its seventy-meter high pinnacle ("le grand rocher") over the green landscape. Like all the other "boulders" that hide the cages, this landmark is man-made, a symbol of artificial nature, erected following the 1931 Colonial Exhibition. The idea once had its charm, but the structures have been pitifully left to dilapidate over the years. More than sixty years old, the Zoo de Vincennes stretches over forty-two acres and ranks among the most popular spots of the capital. Though it still draws families, scientists, ecologists and idlers who have looked elsewhere find it antiquated. No one condemns the animals' living conditions; they seem content and well cared-for. The wild cats' domain, with its characteristic odors, makes some visitors uneasy, but the beasts, well attended by a team of close to forty keepers, don't wander aimlessly about their cages nor do they appear to languish over thoughts of returning to the homeland. The five hundred and fifty mammals and seven hundred birds (both approximate figures) that populate this zoo do not appear to miss their freedom... which, furthermore, many of them never even knew, having come into the world right here in Paris.

Brought in from the polar regions, tropical countries, temperate zones, or born to immigrants, many of these animals are true gourmets, even gluttons, and will plead for snatches of food by "making faces". Top prize in this category goes to the bears, eternal beggars... The zoo asks that the public refrain from overfeeding, especially on Sundays and holidays when swarms of kids (and adults) toss them all sorts of morsels: pieces of bread, peanuts, grains and candy. Once a day, the lions and tigers are fed a hefty meal of twenty-two pounds of raw meat. Most of the other Vincennes boarders, however, gather to be fed twice a day, at designated times and in public view. A fine show that visitors truly appreciate.

FIVE FIFTEEN P.M.

Chocolates at *Angelina*

At *Angelina*'s, the tea is brewed just right; the thick, home-made chocolate, served scalding hot, is famous for its creamy foam… This combined tea room/sweets boutique, truly Parisian, hides its modern-styled elegance behind the arcades of the Rue de Rivoli. Its mostly female clientele will stop here for a light lunch, a perfectly seasoned salad or simply to buy a pastry, preferably a chocolate one. (The *mont-blanc* is marvelously heavy.) But *Angelina* displays its true flavor in mid- and late afternoon, when the ladies and *demoiselles* of all ages and with all their charm, settle in near the gold-decorated columns, in front of the painted landscapes. Those who want to chit-chat in peace and quiet opt for the room at the back.

Angelina ranks among the best known addresses, though it has not always borne that name. Formerly known as *Rumpelmayer's*, this tea-room, legend says, had Marcel Proust as a regular customer; Coco Chanel had her designated table. Rather than catering to nostalgia, *Angelina* welcomes a gentle but steady clientele turnover. It has two clones on the right bank (one in the *Galeries Lafayette* on boulevard Haussmann, the other in the 16th arrondissement), and a smaller version in the *Palais des Congrès*, 17th arrondissement.

Angelina does not hold the monopoly on tea-room buffs. But most rivals are too different to appeal to its clients and draw them away. Among them are the two *Mariage Frères*, marvelously stocked with teas of every possible origin; the cozy *Tea Caddy;* *Carrette*, with crowded terraces on sunny days; *Ladurée* on Rue Royale, with its proud airs of the Second Empire; *Dalloyau*, chic and sober, famous for its light layer cakes and chocolate speciality, *l'opéra*. To continue the inventory in the affluent neighborhoods, whose residents are particularly fussy about where they snack, we mustn't forget *Boissier* and *Coquelin Aîné*, the *Ritz* tea-room, the *Crillon* tea-room (Sonia Rykiel designed their china collection), the majestic hall of the *George V* with its interior garden. Will the young, unconditional fans of Häagen Dazs, some day, when their beauty has matured, prefer *Angelina*'s? They may have to wait for a table.

SIX P.M.

THE OFFICES EMPTY

Specialized sales assistants and clerks glance at their watch: six p.m., one hour to go. Can I help you? Thank you, sir; thank you, ma'am. Hair dressers feel their ankles swell. Bakers will repeat to frustrated clients until seven thirty that they're out of *baguettes*. At six p.m., offices empty, and the cleaning staff, mostly immigrants, moves in. A few executives stay on after their secretaries have left and make sure this is known. The manager is in a meeting with himself, relieving him of the responsibility to think. His secretary lingers, a true executive secretary, better paid than her colleagues but not very well liked.

Model employees, insignificant bosses, accountants, white-collar stuffed shirts, city hall and administrative personnel, apprentices, receptionists with smudged make-up, all surge into the metro at this time of day. Everyone is tired, nobody is pushy. The last ones to board have to squeeze in to make room for the doors to slide shut. A hefty fellow holds the sports journal, *L'Équipe*, folded several times to fit over the shoulder of the blond woman in front of him who gives up on the idea of extricating the magazine from her bag.

A public garden has replaced the Citroën factories. Panhard, the SNECMA, Renault (all heavy industry) have left the city. What remains are the High Executives (capitals intentional), the headquarters personnel, the throngs of civil servants. Paris has been bureaucratized, as was planned. The city built so many offices that some were almost given to Father Pierre, the charismatic priest who has taken the homeless under his protective wing.

The city has become more and more bourgeois, emptying its low-income populations into the outskirts. The metro and RER passengers crowd into the train stations, antechambers of today's remote dormitory-towns. A half-hour, sometimes a full-hour commute, just like this morning... Someday, they will indulge in that promised leisurely visit to the capital to see its museums and monuments. In the meantime, many secretaries have to fetch the baby at the sitter's... in the outskirts, in Vitry or Saint-Ouen, in La Courneuve or Asnière, out where many Parisians live, since the affluent neighborhoods, Passy, Auteuil, La Muette, have the "no vacancy" sign out.

SIX THIRTY P.M.

WORLDLY FLAVORS

Today, there's Alaïa, Lagerfeld, Cioran, Kundera, ben Jelloun, Birkin, Maniatis, Carita, Ouaki, Soto, Lavelli, Noah, Smaïn. Yesterday, and before, there was Reggiani, Ionesco, Picasso, Modigliani, Soutine, Chopin, Huysmans, who was born in Paris but referred to himself as "Dutch, rotted with Parisianism". Need we add Morris (the columns), Wallace (the fountains) and Rothschild (the bank)? The capital's address book, especially since the mid 19th century, is full of names that people have trouble spelling or can't pronounce properly.

Last names with a foreign ring, on shop windows, in the media, imbedded in France's cultural history and on memorial monuments, were often imported one or several generations ago, by exiled nationals or victims of history. Some figure in the social "Who's Who?", others have become simply Parisian. For twenty or thirty years now, Paris has been integrating the patrons of the Passage Brady with its scents of curry, those of the Grande Mosquée tea room, the Greeks that surround the Place Saint-Michel, the Africans, some of whom speak a sophisticated, scholarly French. The Jewish populations from the Sentier, Marais and Belleville, the Moroccan and Tunisian grocers, the Chinese shop-keepers, may all maintain accents, but they adapt faster than some Parisians would adapt to... life in the provinces. For generations, Spanish and Italians have been totally at home in the capital.

Paris is seasoned, colored and invigorated by foreigners who have their stalls, their shops, their restaurants, sometimes even their neighborhoods. They can appear to outnumber Parisians. Welcomed immigrants years ago, today they are taxed of making themselves at home, just as were those, in the late 19th century, who flowed in from the Massif Central, Savoie, Bretagne, Nord and Corsica. These exiles from the provinces, unable to find work as city ditch-diggers, sometimes fell to the ranks of gangsters and prostitutes. Parisians claiming to be of old stock, whose roots may not reach far back, feel sometimes fed up with immigrants. Yet they savor foreign cooking and flavors from elsewhere, so well adapted. Doesn't everyone know how to use chopsticks? Doesn't everyone relish in a *couscous*, a *paella*, a well-made pizza (a rarity), a real or fake lacquered duck? Hasn't everyone at some time been tempted by the abundantly-stocked shop windows, more or less kosher, on Faubourg Montmartre or Rue des Rosiers? Do Parisians really consider Italian restaurants foreign?... (the best of these are not always run by newly-arrived immigrants). It's not unusual to see people feasting on *tapas* (Latin American appetizers) and the classic Belgian combo of steamed muscles and French fries around the Forum des Halles.

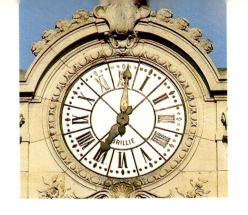

SEVEN P.M.

Boating in the bois de Boulogne

It's a lovely evening of one of spring's longer days... As soon as this season warms the city, the Bois de Boulogne becomes the effervescent scene of bustling activity: from the morning joggers to the evening boaters. The latent rower in every Parisian (a frequent figure in Impressionist paintings and *Belle Époque* photos) realizes just how much muscle it takes to head out on the lake for a casual row, with lover or family, alone or with friends. It may be to whet appetites that people row so avidly in the Bois de Boulogne.

The two lakes spotted with islands are the work of Alphand. This *Polytechnicien* (France's elite engineers), appointed Director of Paris Works at the time of Haussmann's urban rearrangement plan, had a passion for the planning of green zones. In the Bois de Boulogne, he had to rectify the errors of a poorly calculating urban architect, over-zealous to satisfy Napoléon III's desire for a winding river, modelling that of Hyde Park, in this newly arranged open space. This "expert" dug a river of such pronounced slope, that Alphand had to abandon the idea of an artificial river, modifying the plans to comprise two lakes separated by a tall dyke. Running underneath a footbridge, the water cascaded from the upper lake into the lower one... Carrying the project a step further, he had an artesian well dug in Passy to supply the necessary water. This proved insufficient, and water was subsequently drawn off the Canal de l'Ourcq and the Seine to feed the hydraulic system for the Bois de Boulogne.

EIGHT P.M.

AT THE OPÉRA-COMIQUE

The *Opéra Garnier*, facing the city, shows off its splendid architecture. The *Opéra Bastille*, a heavy, contemporary landmark of the renewed eastern sector, sits sternly at the far end of the poorly structured square, under the permanent gaze of the high-perched *Génie de la Liberté*. The *Opéra-Comique*, on the other hand, hides. The "Favart Room", former Italian Room, turns its back to the boulevard, revealing its façade to a small public square with little room to view it in proper perspective. And why? Simply because the singer-comedians of earlier years didn't want to be mistaken for the boulevard jugglers. At the time, the project called for a theater majestically facing the boulevard and standing properly highlighted on the square that was soon to be completed. But the artists demanded that their fief stubbornly turn its back to the street, considered the stage for jugglers and second-rate singers. The tragic fire that erupted during the performance of *Mignon* in 1887 presented an occasion to revise the theater's orientation, but means were insufficient to expropriate the buildings that separated the opera from the boulevard.

The *Opéra-Comique* features works less known to the public, concerts, and original performances, like the *Little Magic Flute* (*Petite Flûte enchantée*). Bold and merry, this version was brought from the *Opéra de Lyon* in early 1995 and revived by the *Ensemble Orchestral de Paris*.
Speaking of which, how would we define the repertoire that attributed the name to this edifice with its caryatids and candelabras? Charles Favart, former pastry-cook turned author and librettist, set the tone originally with lovely light comedies put to music by lesser known composers, as well as those of unequaled prestige, Mozart and Haydn. As the *Opéra-Garnier* held the monopoly on works that were entirely sung, the *Opéra-Comique* had to find its repertoire elsewhere: at first among works that ridiculed true opera and, later, among those that combined sung and spoken dialogue, not unlike operettas. This included the repertoires of Philidor, Grétry, Boeldieu, Adam, Hérold and Aubert, but also *Carmen*... In spite of these restrictions, the *Opéra-Comique* was the first to feature the powerful and "totally musical" work of Puccini, *Tosca*!

EIGHT THIRTY P.M.

BEHIND THE SCENES AT THE *CRAZY HORSE*

Vibrant and charming, though no more provocative in everydaylife than opera ballerinas, the nick-named stars of the *Crazy Horse* are superb on scene when only the stage lights dress their near-nudity. They cannot be compared with earlier strip-tease dancers, in days when the public cringed at a flying brazier or panties. And yet strip-tease was the term used when referring to the show featured on Avenue George-V, world famous for more than thirty years. This was simply for want of a better word to designate the gorgeous ancestors that were Rita Renoir, Yoko Tani, Rita Cadillac and Dodo d'Hambourg, characters of the Parisian night.

Alain Bernardin created the *Crazy Horse Saloon* in 1951... and didn't meet immediate success. He bordered on bankruptcy in his early years with shows featuring the likes of Fernand Raynaud, Charles Aznavour and Georges Wilson. When he took up the premises on the right bank, his cabaret had neither the space nor the cachet that it has today. Unabashed by consequences, Bernardin openly challenged the taboos, aware that the vice-squad could close a cabaret for a fleeting glimpse of a pubis (the strip tease dancers wore triangles adhered with double-faced tape). His audacity paid off, for he claimed fame in the sixties. He continued to defy *convenance*, baring a little more than was permitted, playing with flashing lights, projecting *risqué* silhouettes, preferring the dancer's body to voluptuous anatomies, emphasizing a look or a smile as much as a lower back.

He married Lova Moor who became one of the *Crazy Horse* stars. His style, by then fully developed, was also already widely imitated. The show was fast-moving, preposterous, cinema-like. On the little stage, with the ceiling so low that a *Lido* girl could not stand up, Lova performed alongside Sofia Palladium, as much thoroughbred as Sophia Loren, and a live-in artist. The *Crazy Horse*, just like the *Comédie-Française*, had (and still does) its live-in artists. Among the memorable ones are Trucula Bonbon, Kiki Zanzibar, Lily Paramount and Ulla Starlight. In other cabarets, the pornography can get hard-core or the feathers boring. Alain Bernardin is no longer with us, but the show goes on, perpetuating his characteristic winks.

EIGHT FORTY-FIVE P.M.

EVENING SERVICE AT THE *TOUR D'ARGENT*

"We are at the *Tour d'Argent*... The comedy we will play for you tonight is a dinner party. And I am the restaurant owner. Performing for a different public in a different atmosphere everyday keeps me on my toes for improvisations. The life of the *Tour* changes with the tune of the day and the client's whim." A *gentleman du restaurant* with a world-wide reputation, Claude Terrail "made" the *Tour d'Argent*, recreating and embellishing an institution that first met glory in the 19th century. Today, he is a totally fulfilled prisoner of his institution. Always present, he has hosted Oliver Hardy who brought in the new year with Suzy Delair (without Laurel), Lauren Bacall and Humphrey Bogart, Charlie Chaplin, Orson Welles, the emperor Hiro Hito, Nixon, many presidents and state leaders, all the stars up to the nineties. The *Tour d'Argent*, like the Eiffel Tower, has become a symbol of Paris.

The *Tour*, where Liz Taylor dined with each of her husbands, is the distant descendant of an *auberge* that accommodated Henri III, when the Ile Saint-Louis was no more than an island cow pasture, cut off from the mainland by a stretch of water (the cattle were transported on boats). According to the legend, to be taken lightly, the *auberge* was most respected under the Régence and before the Revolution, at a time when the notion of restaurant, high-grade or not, hardly existed. Its true glory came later, in the 19th century, especially under the excellent management of Frédéric, former *maître d'hôtel* who acquired the restaurant. It was during Frédéric's years that the *Tour* created the famous recipe for *canard au sang* (a duck speciality). Since 1890, every "copy" of this dish has been numbered. The Great Duke Vladimir dined on duckling number 6,043 in 1900. Elizabeth of England was treated to number 185,937 before acceeding to the throne.

Later, Bing Crosby and Frank Sinatra only rarely gave of their songs in restaurants, but they were caught on occasion singing at the end of an evening for the ecstatic guests of the *Tour*. This top-class restaurant, with its bay windows that frame Notre-Dame, the stern of Ile de la Cité and the islands' sky, has its hosts feeling like they're about to step out on stage. The table with the nicest view, in the corner of the room, is reserved long in advance. But the view of Paris (and of the room) is generously provided to everyone. And lovely women can respond to the head manager as did Barbara Hutton one evening when he was unable to seat her at a better table:

"Dear Mr. Terrail, you know quite well that the most beautiful table is always the one at which I am seated!"

NINE P.M.

DINER AT THE *PROCOPE*

The Italian Francesco Procopio dei Coltelli, who started out in Paris serving snacks in a stall at the Saint-Germain fairground, never imagined that his name would one day be immortalized. It was, with the French pronunciation of *Procope*, the name written on the sign of the restaurant he founded, some two hundred odd years ago... The young Sicilian had worked for an Armenian, selling coffee by the cup (a novelty), then, deciding to work for himself, opened his first restaurant on Rue de Tournon. He moved into Rue des Fossés-Saint-Germain (today Rue de l'Ancienne-Comédie) in 1686, elegantly decorated the house with mirrors and chandeliers, attracting the real-tennis fans from across the street. His luck came when the young *Comédie-Française*, located nearby, annexed one of his rooms. Authors, actors and spectators would wander in, drawn by the coffee, sirups, sweets and ice cream.

The restaurant had a solid reputation when its founder passed on in 1716. It prospered under the direction of his son, Alexandre, who attracted such renowned clients as Voltaire (who would write there), Rousseau, Diderot, Beaumarchais, d'Alembert and the other encyclopedists... The Master Zoppi, who managed the *Procope* during the Revolution, won the patronage of Danton, Marat, Camille Desmoulins. He was unable to stop the fervent Hébert from smashing the "table of the reactionaries" that had been so dear to Voltaire. It was repaired and is still there today. Legend tells us that the red bonnet (symbol of the Republic) was exhibited here for the first time.

The *Procope* hosted many of the literary masters of the 19th century, from Balzac to Verlaine. It then declined and fell to the ranks of a refectory. Given another push in the early fifties, its patrons occasionally included Sartre and Beauvoir, before it fell again. A few years ago, Pierre and Jacques Blanc restored and launched it once again. The Blanc brothers, who subsequently acquired the nearby *Arbuci*, are present throughout Paris, running a variety of restaurants: *Grand Café Capucine, La Maison de l'Alsace, Charlot Roi des Coquillages* and the three *Chez Clément*. Francesco Procopio would have envied their expansion, starting with the *Pied de Cochon* which their father, Clément, a wholesale butcher, opened in the days when Parisians flocked to Les Halles to eat succulent meats.

NINE P.M.

THE INVALIDES DOME GOES ABLAZE

The extensive restoration of the monumental Hôtel des Invalides is nearing completion. Ten odd years ago, Louis XIV's enormous and prestigious contribution to the capital's landmarks appeared dirty, dilapidated, almost monotonous, especially in light of the new emphasis on urban restructuring. This museum-monument with its two churches, today still a war veteran's home, hardly glowed any more under the blaze of setting suns, and then slipped, unnoticed, into the evening shadows. With the recent renewal of its gold plating, the dome that majestically crowns the church designed by Jules Hardouin-Mansart is now one of the capital's major landmarks, one of the luminescent jewels of Parisian nights.

Covered with lead, the dome was first gold-plated in 1715. Napoléon I, who would one day lie there to rest in a monumental tomb, had the dome replated. Napoléon III repeated the operation, as did the authorities after the Second World War. By mid-century, though, nothing was left of this precious finery! In 1988, with the approaching festivities for the bicentennial of the French Revolution, François Mitterrand ordered a face-lift for this *chef-d'œuvre* of vast and yet harmonious proportions.

More than twelve kilos of the precious metal were drawn out in sheets of 0.2 micron thickness to cover the lantern and spire, and to return brilliance to the motifs that punctuate the enormous rotund. With the renovations completed in the early nineties, the state allotted several million francs to proper illumination of the jeweled dome and the church's restored façade, leaving the electricity bill to the city of Paris... The sight at night is truly spectacular, especially when viewed from Pont Alexandre-III or from the Avenue de Breteuil.

But the Invalides boasts hoards of visitors in the daytime as well. Having finally recovered its attractive blond pallor, it is further highlighted today by the colors of the revived *jardin de l'Intendant* (Quartermaster's garden). Organized around four interior courtyards which, themselves, surround the majestic *cour d'honneur*, the extensive *Musée de l'Armée* has modernized its displays, giving it a visitor-friendly touch. Amateurs wander among the numerous presentations of weapons and armies of the Ancient Regime, the Revolution, the Empire, the Restauration, the colonial wars, the war of 1870, the two World Wars... Contractors have concurrently renovated the *Musée des Plans-Reliefs* (Museum of topographic maps), situated in the Invalides attics and which authorities threatened for a time to close down. Its extraordinary models of forts, citadels and their likes were almost shipped to Lille. To sum up the Invalides, it's once again the grandiose monument it was meant to be, ready now for the year 2000.

NINE P.M.

AT THE TUILERIES

The presence of an amusement park in the Tuileries, once reserved to the noble, today the archetype of public gardens, is highly controversial. But Parisians have a weakness for the Ferris wheel, spectacular in its delicacy. In the daytime, for the visitor leaving the Louvre pyramid, it tactfully fits in between the Arc de Triomphe du Carrousel and the Rue de Rivoli. In the evening, it stands like a giant jewel, most noticeable, but not overly gaudy.

The Tuileries' general appearance has changed very little in the past hundred years. However, its rejuvenescence, now nearing completion, was years in coming. Interestingly enough, those who violently opposed the opening of an amusement park, did not protest against the deterioration and defacing of the garden's river side. Parisians obsessed with the Tuileries' appearance on the Carrousel and Rivoli side have little or no concern for the garden's harmony with the bordering Seine. Renovation of certain areas of the vast garden, the fate of the assembly of statues and the future reserved to the Esplanade des Feuillants are matters of great concern and provoke heated disagreement. But people tend to forget that the terrace on the Seine banks (Terrasse du Bord de l'Eau), visited only by enlightened tourists, affords one of the most splendid panoramic views of the river and an extraordinary frontal view of the Musée d'Orsay and the Hôtel de Salm. In spite of the traffic which the tunnel swallows up a few hundred meters too late, the Tuileries is as much a lovely garden on the banks of the Seine as it is a monumental courtyard for the Grand Louvre!

The Ferris wheel, a familiar sight in the daytime, unique at night, stands up tall on the Terrasse des Feuillants where it encloses in luminous circles the Place de la Concorde, on a line between the Champs-Elysées and the Tuileries.

TEN P.M.

The Bateaux-Mouches light up the banks

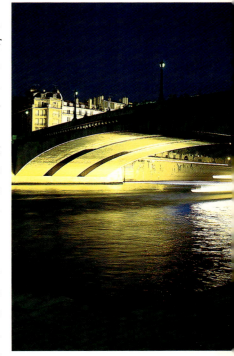

The Seine of boatmen, poets and lovers molded Paris, who then took possession of its banks, designed its island and dotted it here and there with bridges. In spite of incessant modifications in urban landscaping and population shuffling, the capital today is still defined in terms of the river, even simply in the persistent, though often unclear, opposition between "right bank" and "left bank." An entire tourist flotilla navigates the stretch from the banks of the Eiffel Tower to the stern of the Ile Saint-Louis, delighting visitors with most of the capital's best views. And at nighttime, their projectors light up the monument façades that the city has left in the dark. (Not until the mid nineties were bridges properly fitted out with esthetic lighting).

At nightfall, projectors from the larger panoramic flatboats reveal breath-taking sights on the banks: the Musée d'Orsay, the Louvre, Notre-Dame, the Conciergerie. The lights illuminate walls that are otherwise silent in their darkness, big segments of history, banks tastefully tailored or brutally modernized by the hideous express lane. With the exception of the Eiffel Tower, the Invalides dome and the few monuments highlighted by projectors, Paris remains a rather dark city at night. The capital owes, in part, its nickname of the City of Light to the "commercial" lighting of the Bateaux-Mouches. Climb aboard and discover its treasures, eternal in the briefly parted shadows.

People have been boarding Bateau-Mouches to see the heart of historic Paris for more than a century. The "Company of shuttle steamboats" won recognition in Lyon, launching onto the Saône propeller boats built on the Mouche boatyard. When the Suresnes damn finally stabilized the Seine water-level in the capital, the Lyon Company received the green light, at the eve of the 1867 World's Fair, to commercialize boats modelled on the Mouche. Several other shuttle navigation companies emerged, uniting finally in 1886 to form the *Compagnie générale des bateaux parisiens*, whose 107 boats counted a total of 27,000 seats. During the *Belle Époque*, millions of Parisians and tourists came to realize, as they slipped down the avenue of water, that Paris had been created by the Seine.

TEN P.M.

INTERMISSION AT *FOLIES-BERGÈRE*

Where, exactly, was the bar at the *Folies-Bergère*, its huge mirror filled with dark and blond reflections, that Edouard Manet exposed at the 1882 Paris salon? The painting is famous, but neither the collaborators of Madame Martini, "night empress" who resumed control of the club in 1974, nor savvy art critiques, could determine the exact perspective from where the artist worked. Did he invent this perspective for a rendition truer than life? Today, no one sitting at the present bar during intermission really cares.

Fou des Folies, Folies, je t'adore, Folies de Paris... Whether conventional, with gaudy jewelry and sequins, or truly contemporary, with the necessary allusions to Paris' eternal nights, the spectacular shows at *Folies-Bergère* play on and on. Every so often, a special series of performances will interrupt the house repertoire, showing as long as there's public demand. This was the case for *Les Années Twist* (The Twist Years), featuring 260 tunes of the sixties, relived twenty-five years later in a retro-style musical.

The renovated *Folies-Bergère*, determined to appear contemporary, is nonetheless more than one hundred years old. Guy de Maupassant, whose heroines of *Bel Ami* lived in the 9th arrondissement, marveled at the colossal *promenoir* (a sort of walkway that attracted crowds during intermission) which pleasure-seeking literature depicted with more accuracy than did Manet. Below Montmartre, the colorful arena of parties and party-goers, socialites and prostitutes, coarse songs and raucous rhymes, the *Folies-Bergère* was famous long before Maurice Chevalier landed his legendary contract there in 1907. Toulouse-Lautrec, a regular at the *Moulin-Rouge*, often attended shows. He enjoyed the brilliant novelties imported from America, still called the New World; he loved Loïe Fuller's dances, Little Tich's odd numbers that ingeniously played upon the flaws of her midget body. On the *promenoir*, high-class prostitutes rubbed shoulders with snobby socialites and gentlemen sporting their decoration of honor. But the *Folies-Bergère* had high standards. Whores wandering in from the Place Blanche were invited to head over to the *Moulin-Rouge*.

At the close of the 19th century, the *Folies-Bergère* set the tone, starting a cultural phenomenon later picked up at the *Moulin-Rouge, Casino de Paris* and the *café-concerts*. In *Ma Route et mes chansons* (My road and my songs), Maurice Chevalier remembers the event that led to his contract with *Folies-Bergère*. Starting out among the "honky-tonks" of Belleville, he sang at the *Casino de Montmartre, La Fourmi, La Scala* and *L'Eldorado*, as well as at the famous *Alcazar* in Marseille...

ELEVEN P.M.

ROAD WORK ON THE BANKS

Parisians - or rather Parisian drivers - are past masters in the art of bellyaching about public works. They enthusiastically applaud urban restructuring (at its completion!), and holler at the lack of maintenance... The capital's Department of Road Works faces the formidable challenge of overseeing nearly 1,580 kilometers of public roads, identified by 70,000 street signs, not always very legible. Among these are occasional strange names, recalling an old store or café, former proprietors, convents or other edifices that have since disappeared: Rue de la Lune, Rue du Moulin-de-la-Vierge, Rue des Blancs-Manteaux... 41,000 street signs of prescribed color and dimensions, more than 8,000 traffic lights, around 500 well-defined arrondissement maps and a dozen "tourist maps" all allow the capital's drivers and pedestrians to find their way through the 8,000 intersections and 6,000 crossroads.

Every Parisian's nightmare is to see traffic brought to a stop. And it happens, from nine p.m. on, maybe for the night, maybe for several days, usually in the slack summer season, but very possibly at any time, especially in the case of an emergency. Traffic can be stopped for everyday cleaning or a major spruce-up, for resurfacing, or repairs on the network of city gas, water, and telephone lines. It can be stopped for the opening of a new route, the construction of a bridge or walkway, the improvements of an area around a station on the new Eole and Météor RATP lines (just nearing completion)... Minute coordination here is imperative! These urban operations are concerns of top priority; it's nonetheless difficult to forbid to the motorized masses access to even one lane of Paris' congested Boulevards des Maréchaux (33.7 kilometers), Boulevard Périphérique (35 kilometers) or right-bank express lane (13 kilometers).

ELEVEN P.M.

THE LOUVRE DOZES

As a project started under the kings, continued under the Republic, the Louvre finally became *le Grand Louvre* after eight centuries of construction, extensions and reorganization. The first major decision-maker, Philippe Auguste, was followed by Charles V (first sculptured décors), Henri IV (Grande Galerie), Louis XIII (Pavillon de l'Horloge), Louis XIV (Galerie d'Apollon), Louis XV (Cour Carrée), Napoléon I (expansion of the museum), Napoléon III (Salle du Manège), and François Mitterrand (Pyramid, new Richelieu wing). This palace museum, that was once a solemn, uninviting edifice, sullen in spite of its fame, where close to a thousand people work, where some days, up to thirty thousand visitors pass through, has today become an open "city". Even after hours, when the Pyramid will allow only the cleaning staff in, the new Louvre is a sight to behold. Through the enormous windows of the Passage Richelieu, one can admire the spectacular sculptures in the Marly and Puget courtyards.

Finally rid of the age-old dirt, the museum, now air-conditioned and excellently lit, has doubled its surface. It is hailed today as the biggest in the world, though authorities of the New York Metropolitan Museum may not agree. It is also a complex administrative machine, run by great art connoisseurs as well as competent finance managers. The palace-museum lives twenty-four hours a day. The guards, or rather, superintendents, are present day and night, in smaller numbers on the quiet Tuesday evenings, when the uniformed squads wax the floors, clean the windows, dust the marble surfaces, replace burnt-out light bulbs...

MIDNIGHT

Sorting the Mail

The postal service employs nineteen thousand agents in Paris, some visible to the public from behind their windows or working in the background, others working during the open hours or non-stop in rotating teams, in premises of every imaginable size, from a tiny cubicle to the gigantic hall. Everyday, six million items: letters, third-class envelopes and other parcels, leave Paris through the mail, via the 179 offices (which service 200,000 people daily) and the 2,000 yellow public mailboxes.

The enormous mass of mail, that used to fill thousands of leather bags, today is "containerized", facilitating the handling in train stations and airports. Stamped letters, destined to the suburbs, the provinces and abroad, are distributed to eight sorting centers throughout the capital. The postal service divided Paris up with respect to the number of letters collected and local traffic problems. This explains why some arrondissements are assigned to two different centers, while others receive mail sorted in a different arrondissement.

More than five million letters and parcels, having traveled the reverse route, are delivered in the morning to the *concierges*'s flat, in personalized mailboxes or dropped off at companies and corporations. Not far from Boulevard Richard-Lenoir, the Paris XI-Popincourt Center, which distributes for the 11th arrondissement, sorts 300,000 items daily. Over 300 people work here, relaying one another almost 24 hours a day. A team of 200 postmen and women will then take the mail to final destinations between 8:30 a.m. and 5:30 p.m.

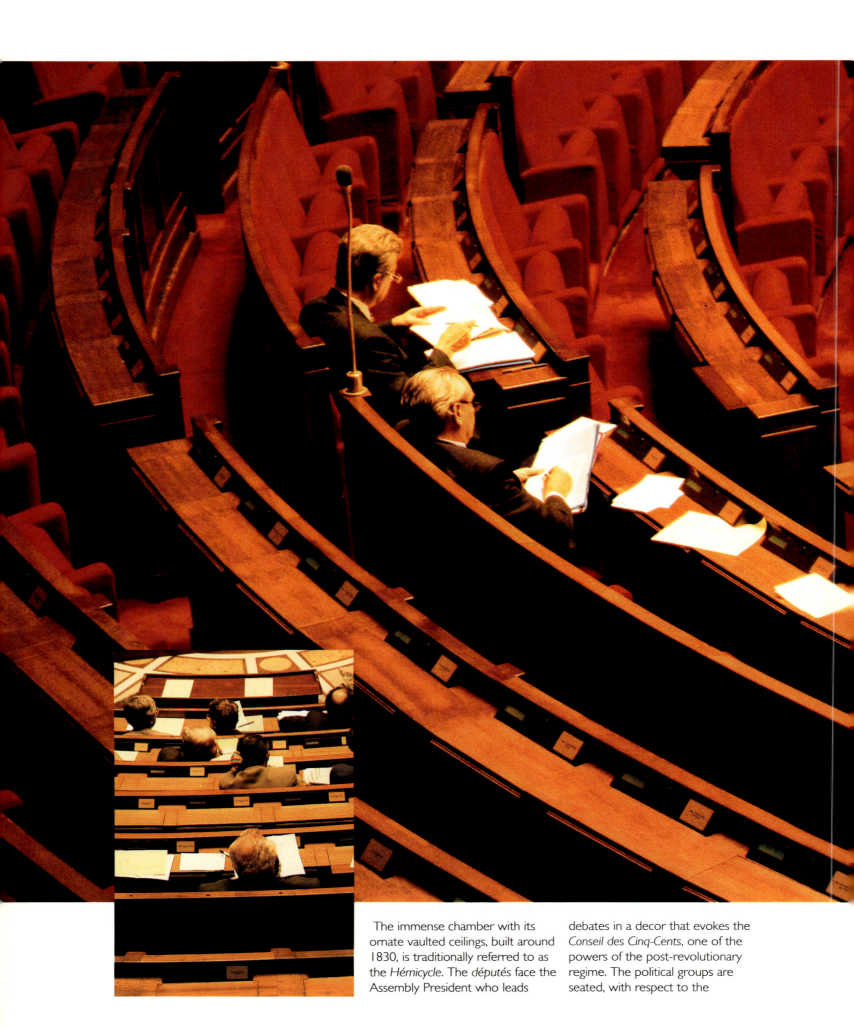

The immense chamber with its ornate vaulted ceilings, built around 1830, is traditionally referred to as the *Hémicycle*. The *députés* face the Assembly President who leads debates in a decor that evokes the *Conseil des Cinq-Cents*, one of the powers of the post-revolutionary regime. The political groups are seated, with respect to the

TWELVE THIRTY A.M.

NIGHT SESSION AT THE *ASSEMBLÉE NATIONALE*

Elected by the people, working for the people, France's *députés* (national assemblymen and women) must oftentimes debate for long hours. These officials can, and do, fall behind in their sleep. Night session attendance is mandatory, yet many seats remain empty, when the debated issue lacks luster or when no one takes roll. Parisians forgive representatives of the nation for not always demonstrating enthusiasm in their assignments. They make no issue of an *Hémicycle* (national assembly room) nearly empty at ungodly hours.

Furthermore, though they could, the public doesn't flock to the Palais-Bourbon for night sessions any more than do the *députés*. Any citizen may enter the *Hémicycle* by obtaining an entry card from the attendant or from a *député*. One gains access to the assembly hall through the *cour d'honneur* on the side opposite that of the Seine. The side that faces the Concorde, reflecting the columns of the Madeleine, is simply a majestic, decorative façade.

The Palais-Bourbon was built for the legitimized daughter of Louis XIV and Madame de Montespan. Until the 19th century, the *Hémicycle*, located in the heart of the Palace, was a salon where exquisite duchesses conversed with young marquis. Today, the *députés* listen, hail one another, shout abuses, applaud and vote, for the benefit of the nation, in a sumptuous chamber with marble ionic columns. These officials reflect and debate under the historic paintings of the conference hall and in the lounges which, together, constitute the *couloirs* (hallways) of the *Assemblée nationale*.

president, on the left, in the center, or on the right. The effigies representing Liberty, Public Order, Wisdom, Justice, Prudence... remind the speakers of the virtues of a republican democracy.

ONE A.M.

THE EIFFEL TOWER TURNS IN FOR THE NIGHT

One o'clock: Paris' most beautiful candelabra goes out: the Eiffel Tower, the shepherdess of the bridges below and the clouds above, at night becomes the capital's quiet fairy. A silhouette that the foggy darkness sometimes steals from the city. The young centenarian, colossal and delicately spider-like, has stirred Parisians ever since her construction for the 1889 World's Fair. She momentarily lost center stage when the brand new Pompidou Center and Forum des Halles stole public attention. But she won back her place in Parisians' hearts when the new lighting scheme transformed her into a jewel. The Tower that towers over all towers, without dwarfing or shadowing anything, passes from one generation to another, maintaining its youth. When she suffered some rusting, a team of acrobatic painters touched her up. When she looked too weighty, sky mechanics relieved her of 1,300 tons of unnecessary metal additions. She has grown taller, but no one resents the twenty additional meters permitting the installation of a television antenna. Quite the contrary. Parisians are grateful to their sentinel for being useful, for relaying waves, for holding an array of apparatus that measure the wind, the air and the weather.

How could poets and writers, even the most contemporary, even the most *avant-garde*, have insulted as some did this marvelous structure of knitted steel, so gentle against the sky, never hiding the sun? Paul Gauguin marveled at what he called "gothic iron lace" in the Tower. But Léon Bloy spoke of a "truly tragic lamp" and Paul Verlaine of a "belfry's skeleton." During its construction, Alexandre Dumas, Guy de Maupassant and several artists signed a letter of protest, seeking to prevent "the abominable column of bolted sheet-metal" from humiliating the historic monuments of a city that belongs to the exalted gothics, to the likes of Jean Goujon and Pierre Lescot.

ONE FIFTEEN A.M.

Supper at the *Ritz-Club*

It's not unusual for the festive French to have "supper" (as opposed to dinner) at this late hour... *L'Espadon,* a top-grade restaurant on the main patio of the *Ritz,* turns people away after eleven p.m. But those determined to dine can find a table by using connections or sweet-talking their way into the *Ritz-Club* (jacket a must, tie highly recommended). You can reach this discotheque, complete with lounges and a restaurant, from the Place Vendôme, following an endless corridor. Or, from the Rue Cambon, you can descend directly into the luxurious darkness, thus bypassing the gold and crystal-decked hotel, founded by César Ritz in 1878, where the shadows of Coco Chanel and Ernest Hemingway still lurk.

Though Parisian nights are not what they used to be, they continue to tingle with some excitement. The manager of the *Ritz-Club,* a former bigwig at *Castel,* was the first to create a true club underneath a luxury hotel, catering to its affluent clientele, to wealthy Parisians, posh and proper provincials... and, quite often, culinary buffs. When top-notch restaurateurs and chefs meet in Paris, they regularly pay their respects to Michel Gaubert, in charge here until daybreak.

Guy Legay, one of Paris' most renowned cooks and member of the elitist association *Traditions & Qualité,* composed the menu, accommodating clients' appetites regardless of the hour. The choices include a few deliciously rustic dishes and two or three lighter, more refined ones. Even in the elegant light and shade of this famous hotel, one can eat after midnight, answering to any whim, including a craving for French-fries. At night, the cream of society has every right...

Michel Gaubert (second from left) is one of Paris' nighttime workers. Here, Valérie Vrinat (daughter of Claude Vrinat, of Taillevent) has persuaded him to join her family at the table for a brief moment. The Vrinat family visits one cellar after another; they watch over the 40,000 bottles of the Taillevent cellars on Rue du Faubourg-Saint-Honoré.

TWO A.M.

THE ROTARY PRESSES SPIN

We're in Saint-Ouen. Not far from the Pleyel tower, a few kilometers from Sacré-Cœur, *Le Parisien* is coming off the press. There's a familiar smell of fresh ink prevails, from midnight to three a.m., along with the heavy vibration of the five printing presses spinning out their 45,000 copies an hour. Not record-breaking, but fast enough to allow the well-read daily, featuring general news, to reach the vendor stalls on time. *L'Équipe*, a sports daily, spins off two other presses nearby. Together, this represents a hundred tons of paper, permeated with news, essential or not, but always the latest... In today's age of computers and suburban relocation, Paris no longer has a "press district". The dailies, weeklies, and monthlies have all left the center city, following the whole-salers of Les Halles.

Today, it's hard to imagine the heavy presses hammering basements of the Rue du Louvre, the Rue du Croissant and the Rue Réaumur. For more than a century, reporters, editorialists, editing secretaries, linotypists and printers gathered in neighborhoods of the 2nd arrondissement. Day and night, they would fill these streets with life, strolling up and down the Grands Boulevards, spending long hours in quaint cafés that never closed. The very first edition of the morning dailies, destined for the provinces, would come off the press at around half-past midnight. It would leave immediately, typos included, for the distribution points. The second edition, its first page modified with updates or scoops, would arrive for the early-risers' breakfast. Occasional special editions would appear, sometimes upstaged by the first editions of the evening press. Daytime readers haven't noticed the changes. But the night-owls who knew this area when Les Halles was still part of the landscape, remember the delivery vehicles loading stories of the world just as the fruit and vegetable trucks pulled in...

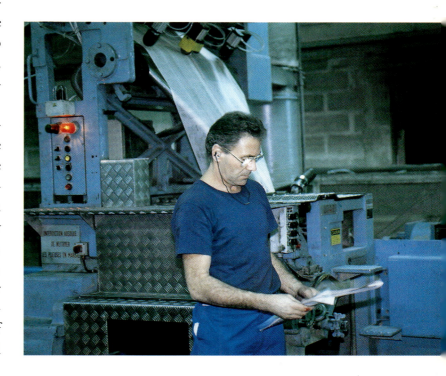

THREE A.M.

NIGHT-OWLS AND NIGHT BUSES

Late-night party-goers, sometimes limited in numbers (it's not new year's eve everyday, and the week has only one Saturday...), hail a taxi or drive home. The night-workers, in higher numbers but with lower salaries, must often settle for public transportation. Since the last metro crosses Paris at quarter to one, this means taking the bus. The limited network at this time of night leaves some districts completely unserviced. The 15th arrondissement, with its partially low-income population, is one of these; the Passy-Auteuil neighborhood is another, but that population can afford to ignore public transportation, even when it works.

The emblem of a little owl, perched in front of a full moon, marks the ten bus lines of the *Noctambus*. They all leave from the Place du Châtelet, said to be the network's navel of the city at nighttime. Of the two lines that cross the Seine, one goes well beyond the Porte d'Italie. Passing through Kremlin-Bicêtre, it services the fishmongers' hanger at Rungis, bustling with activity from two a.m. The lines A and H (numbers designate daytime lines, most of which run until 8:30 p.m., some until 12:30 a.m.) cover the route of metro line number one and RER line A, the former extending to La Défense, the latter as far as Château de Vincennes. At this hour, suburbanites heading home to Montreuil, Pantin, Clichy or Levallois, as well as those who live on the road leading to Rungis are lucky: they have a bus every hour from 1:30 to 5:30 a.m. Those who live elsewhere must wait for the vast urban machinery to kick into gear. But are there many of them? Paris doesn't seem to live, work, and play by night as it used to. Tourists on the last metro may think they're leaving the party early; they needn't worry. When the monument lights go out, most of Paris is already sound asleep, and the city is losing momentum. Only those that have to are still out there moving about... Should Boris Vian and the night-owls of the fifties return, they would head off to Barcelone, Madrid or New York where the midnight sun still shines.

FOUR A.M.

THE FIRST BATCH

Just as the beret does not distinguish the French, the *baguette* does not distinguish Parisians. It does, nonetheless, symbolize daily life in the capital. Clients are often seen breaking off the end as they exit the bakery, savoring a warm, fresh bite on their way home (a good *baguette* always arrives home, at least a quarter of it already eaten). And yet the *baguette* cannot unduly brag about its gastronomic virtues. Its occasionally hard crust usually hides insipid dough, unworthy of a tasty dish.

In spite of the *baguette*'s significance, Parisian bakers, both talented and mediocre, have widely diversified their production, now selling *ficelle* (half of the *baguette*), *flûte* (smaller version of *baguette*), *boule* (round loaf), *campagne* (farmhouse bread), *épis* (spiked loaf), *tresse* (braided loaf), breads said to be "special", made with bran or with various different grains, and the ultimately ludicrous "bio" breads (no additives)... This diversity, some say purely for show, proves nonetheless that bread has kept its place of priority on tables, justifiably or not, in a city where bakers have constituted a recognized trade since the days of Saint Louis.

Some say, "there's nothing simpler than good bread". It would be an unfair exaggeration to add "nothing scarcer either". Every arrondissement in Paris counts two or three excellent bakeries, easy to spot by the lines that form at the door off and on throughout the day, from 7 a.m. to 8 p.m.

Not all bakers have a genius for bread. Unlike that of a pastry-cook, this trade is relatively easy to learn; it does, however, call for a certain inclination. Many "bakeries" are simply *dépôts*, selling bread delivered from factories... but some people don't seem to care. It's fair to say that the best bakers round up the best clientele! The Poilâne brothers, who work separately though they share some old secrets, are among those who contend that the baker can maintain client loyalty without having to diversify and "gadgetize" the trade. One could almost find fault with the monotony of their production... This photograph was taken in Max Poilâne's bakery, less commercialized than his brother, though a recognized and appreciated artisan. One could question the affirmation that today's bread must be baked in wood-burning ovens. Often kneaded in the middle of the night, it does just as well cooked in electric ovens. Whatever the cooking method, what matters here is the baker's feeling and love for his trade.

Paris has become a city of executives and white-collar workers (not all of whom have the privilege of living here). The capital undoubtedly boasts more doctors, lawyers and pharmacists than baker's boys. But bakers and those who sell their goods at the market, are still around to give Paris a true soul. It's four a.m.; we've completed the cycle. The night is coming to a close, the morning will soon be upon the city. Does the day look promising? We'll get back to that...

5:00 a.m.   Gare de Lyon belfry clock

6:00 a.m.   The Conciergerie

7:00 a.m.   6 Rue de Sèvres

8:00 a.m.   Hôpital Cochin

9:00 a.m.   Jardin des Plantes

10:00 a.m.   Gare du Nord

11:00 a.m.   Hôpital Rothschild

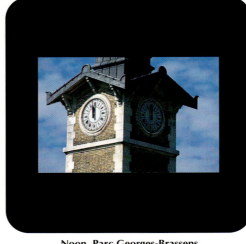
Noon. Parc Georges-Brassens

1:00 p.m.   Assemblée nationale

2:00 p.m.   134 Rue Réaumur

3:00 p.m.   Ministère de la Défense

4:00 p.m.   Église Saint-Thomas-d'Aquin

5:00 p.m.   Église de la Trinité

6:00 p.m.   Rue Monge

7:00 p.m.   Gare des Invalides

8:00 p.m.   Gare d'Austerlitz

9:00 p.m.   Musée du Louvre

10:00 p.m.   Musée d'Orsay

11:00 p.m.   Boulevard Saint-Michel

Midnight. Hôtel de Ville

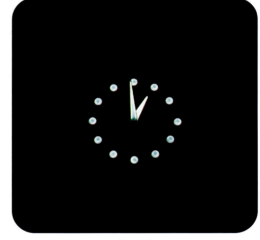
1:00 a.m.   Gare Montparnasse

2:00 a.m.   Avenue de l'Opéra

3:00 a.m.   Gare Saint-Lazare

4 a.m.   Gare du Nord

Aknowledgements

M. Montes (RATP)
Mme Balsan (crèmerie des Carmes, place Maubert)
M. et Mme Dont (maison Le Cuvier, place Maubert)
Évelyne (Moulié, place du Palais-Bourbon)
Sergent Yannick Tœuf et Commandant Étienne Grech (Garde républicaine)
Ambassade d'Auvergne
M. Biby (musée Grévin)
Carré des Feuillants
Joël Robuchon
Guy Savoy
Bouillon Chartier
Bibliothèque Sainte-Geneviève
Alain Gallet, newspaper delivery man
Angelina
Tang frères
Izraël (rue François-Miron)
Opéra-Comique
Polly Harper (Crazy Horse Saloon)
Tour d'Argent
Procope
Folies-Bergère
La Poste Paris XI-Popincourt
Sophie Michel (Assemblée nationale)
Michel Gaubert (Ritz-Club)
Le Parisien
Max Poilâne
Pat Short
Bernard, Mélanie, Martin, Benjamin

Photographs

Jacques-Louis Delpal : pages 48-49, 58, 60-61.

Jacques Lebar : pages 10-11, 16-17, 18-19, 21, 24-25, 27, 28, 29 (above), 31, 33, 38-39, 41, 51 (below), 54-55, 56-57, 59, 62-63, 70-71, 72-73, 74-75, 96-97
and clocks from 6:00 a.m. to 7:00 p.m.

Martine Mouchy : pages 4, 6-7, 9, 13, 15, 22-23, 29 (below), 30, 34-35, 42-43, 51 (above), 52-53, 65, 66-67, 69, 77, 78-79, 82-83, 87, 88-89, 90-91, 92-93, 94-95, 98-99, 100-101, 102-103, 104-105, 106-107, 109, 112-113, 115, 117
and clocks from 8:00 p.m. to 5:00 a.m.

Christian Sarramon : pages 36-37, 44-45, 47 (above left ; below), 81, 84, 110-111.

Collection Guy Savoy : page 47 (above right).

Mise en page : Fabienne Vaslet, Parigramme, avec l'aide amicale d'Isabelle Chemin
Photogravure Euresys, à Baisieux
Flashage Leyre, à Paris
Imprimé en Italie

ISBN : 2-84096-037-0
Dépôt légal : mars 1995